4-D BRANDING

4-D BRANDING

Cracking the corporate code of the network economy

Thomas Gad

with a foreword by Richard Branson

FINANCIAL TIMES
Prentice Hall

An imprint of **Pearson Education**

London · New York · San Francisco · Toronto · Sydney
Tokyo · Singapore · Hong Kong · Cape Town · Madrid
Paris · Milan · Munich · Amsterdam

PEARSON EDUCATION LIMITED

Head Office:
Edinburgh Gate
Harlow CM20 2JE
Tel: +44 (0)1279 623623
Fax: +44 (0)1279 431059

London Office:
128 Long Acre
London WC2E 9AN
Tel: +44 (0)20 7447 2000
Fax: +44 (0)20 7240 5771
Website: www.business-minds.com

First published in Great Britain in 2001
Published in Sweden in 2000 by
Bookhouse Publishing AB

© Bookhouse Publishing AB 2001

The right of Thomas Gad to be identified as Author
of this Work has been asserted by him in accordance
with the Copyright, Designs and Patents Act 1988.

ISBN 0 273 65368 7

British Library Cataloguing in Publication Data
A CIP catalogue record for this book can be obtained from the British Library

10 9 8 7 6 5 4 3 2 1

Typest by Pantek Arts Ltd, Maidstone, Kent
Printed and bound in Great Britain by Biddles Ltd, Guildford and King's Lynn

The Publishers' policy is to use paper manufactured from sustainable forests.

Contents

Foreword

BRANDS ARE POWERFUL WEAPONS changing the entire landscape of industries. They are a transforming commercial force. 'Today brands are everything, and all kinds of products and services – from accounting firms to sneaker makers to restaurants – are figuring out how to transcend the narrow boundaries of their categories and become a brand surrounded by a Tommy Hilfiger-like buzz,' says the American guru Tom Peters.

The trouble is that many organizations continue to think of brands in traditional terms. When they think of brands, they think in one dimension; they think of commercial expediency. As Thomas Gad points out in *4-D Branding*, branding in the twenty-first century requires sensitivity and imagination. Great brands touch people. One-dimensional branding has to give way to four-dimensional branding.

Branding in four dimensions is concerned with building and sustaining relationships. Relationships are the key to commercial success. Bonds unite us. A recent definition of branding, by three American consultants, describes it as 'creating a mutually acknowledged relationship between the supplier and buyer that transcends isolated transactions or specific individuals.' Brands are now pinned around a relationship rather than a product.

And the more personal the relationship the better. The great brands strike a personal chord with you. They make you feel better, different, bigger, smaller, happier, more comfortable, warmer, more confident. They reach parts other brands only dream about. From being physical, brands have become psychological. Brands are about hearts and minds, feelings and emotions. They touch us.

They do so because they are associated with values with which we identify. Increasingly, brands are driven by values. Great brands stand for something, something which people believe in and which matters to them. Values and brands are inextricably linked.

To build sensitive brands with strong, persuasive and long-lasting values is far from easy. For every branding success there are a great many failures. Relationships are not quickly or easily built. You can't fake them. Values cannot be speedily forgotten if it is inconvenient or commercially expedient. Values have to have meaning and longevity; otherwise they are valueless. You cannot embrace innovation up to a point or only sometimes. Branding demands commitment: commitment to continual re-invention, striking chords with people to stir their emotions, and commitment to imagination. It is easy to be cynical about such things, much harder to be successful.

Success, however, is not an accidental commercial freak. Thankfully, management tools are now available which make managing, creating and nurturing powerful brands more achievable than ever before. In *4-D Branding*, Thomas Gad lays the groundwork for understanding how brands really do work and presents tools for managers which are easily understood but which work. His message, and the growing power of branding, demands recognition, no matter what your business.

Sir Richard Branson
London, December 2000

Preface

SAY THE WORD 'branding' and it is like a magical incantation. A veil of commercial karma, reassurance as the logos of fast-moving consumer brands pass before your eyes: Coca-Cola, Heineken, Marlboro, Nescafé. Their names and images are magical, but there is no sleight of hand at work, no David Copperfield lurking with a sword, a ready smile, and a bucket of dry ice. This is magic created through years of painstaking work and piles of dollar bills invested in ad campaigns on expensive media such as television.

Trouble is, the magic is wearing off. Exit magician stage right. The 1950s, when the modern concept of branding was born and put into action, are now a distant memory. Gone are the days of corporate man and dutiful woman, 2.2 children, a house with a picket fence, and fulfilment through copious consumption and the acquisition of material possessions. The world has changed – and that includes the world of brands.

Today, brands are not the preserve of the marketing department. Brands are too important to be left to the marketing department – or any other 'department,' come to that. Organizational ghettoes do not create vibrant, world-changing brands.

Indeed, the contemporary brand – and the brand of the future – is about much more than marketing. A new art of branding is beginning to develop. This focuses on the brand as a management tool; a tool used in marketing, but also throughout the organization and beyond; a tool encompassing dealers, suppliers, investors, and customers.

The use of branding as a management tool means that branding is no longer restricted to consumer businesses. It is now of huge and growing importance in the business-to-business sector, in the production and selling of knowledge-based services, and in virtually every other industrial or business classification.

The impact of brands is now manifest in every single aspect of business life, from the smallest decision in the corner store to the biggest decision in the largest company. Inside and outside the organization, the brand is all-embracing. It touches all of our business activities. The brand is a packaging device. It delivers, in a very concentrated form, a business vision, business plan, corporate culture, image, and many more aspects of business life that were previously conceptually compartmentalized. Brands are increasingly important in all our working lives. That means that every one of us needs an understanding of what branding really is. Whether you work in its traditional stronghold of marketing, or in finance, IT, or human resources, branding will increasingly affect you. If you're one of the pioneers of the Network Economy, it will be absolutely critical to your success. In the cacophonous online world, your brand filters out your message from all the other noise.

The influence of branding is also growing outside the vibrant Network Economy. As well as being important to a variety of stakeholders in the business, branding is vital to a company's performance on the financial markets. The brand is now a highly valuable asset. In 1988, British foods company RHM (Rank Hovis McDougall) made history by becoming the first firm to include a brand valuation on its balance sheet – attaching an asset value to its brands. The brand is now becoming the dominant component in the financial valuation of any enterprise.

Indeed, I believe the brand is now a more important corporate driver than profit. After all, who is turned on by profit? Executives care about their share options, but they are alone in their passion. Customers and employees (unless they share significantly in the spoils) are left cold by talk of profits. When you buy something, do you care how profitable the manufacturer is?

This, I know, is heresy. Profits have ruled the corporate world since time immemorial, and of course they are important. But the most valid reason for choosing a driver other than profit is that profit is not unique to your company. What is the difference between two companies in the same market with the same levels of profit? All dollar bills are created equal – brands thrive on difference. It is difference that gives competitive advantage.

The modern concept of the brand is far removed from that understood in the past. Branding is all about uniqueness. In this age of sameness, difference rules. The brand, as I define it, is your company's differentiation code. It is a code as vital, as powerful, as universal, and as unique as DNA.

The vast majority of the DNA code in human beings is identical. Difference is created by a very small percentage of our personal DNA. This is also the case with most products, services, and companies. There are very small differences between competitors in most businesses. The similarities are much greater than the differences. But a small amount of differentiation is enough not only to produce very different human personalities, but also to do the same with branded products, services, and companies.

4-D Branding aims to enable you to reach a full understanding of your brand's differentiation code and to make it work for you immediately.

4-D Branding is not a catch-all, abstract concept. There need not be anything vague about it. The brand can be precisely defined. The exact scope and specifications of its design, attitude, daily routines, and activities can be clearly established. If you achieve this, you can begin to build a brand that lasts – one that endures.

Today's brand builders have to create brands that can survive for the next five, ten, fifteen years. That will not be easy and many will fall by the wayside. Look at Levis. Yesterday's branding icon is now struggling to survive and to reinvent itself for changing times. Brand builders cannot afford to ignore the future. Indeed, they have to build today with the future in mind. The future is treacherous, unpredictable, and uncertain, but it is there to be seized and shaped. The future must be built into the brand.

My basic premise is that you – not an expensive consultant or a smart academic – are the person best able to construct the future of your business. You know your business best, and you have to learn to understand and manage your brand. You have to take responsibility for its long-term welfare.

If you are a leading actor in your marketplace, you will be actively shaping your future – at least the next three to five years. Looking further out, the future takes on a more elusive shape. Longer-term trends in society require the creative inspiration of artists, writers, and similar people.

This book explains a method that enables you to futurize your brand. It forces you to develop sides of your brand that would never be explored in a classic media situation. It requires personalized, intimate, and interactive communication, brand storytelling, and philosophizing. This is in total contrast to the mass marketing era, when a brand builder could get away with cosmetic superficiality. There is nothing superficial, trite or frivolous in truly, deeply, understanding your brand.

Today your brand has to have the qualities of a dear friend, someone you really trust (and I mean *really*). You should be able to shop for a product or a service, whether over the Net or down the shopping mall, and feel totally safe with what you are getting, seeing, buying, and experiencing. A brand should be something you relish listening to, a source of entertainment, and something connecting you with other people, forming a social community around the brand.

4-D Branding is as an introduction to systematically engineering this new kind of future-oriented management through branding. At every stage, I have aimed to make the book both simple and practical. Read it and reap.

Thomas Gad
Stockholm, December 2000

Acknowledgments

THIS BOOK IS BUILT on nearly 20 years' experience of communication and branding in the advertising industry. So, acknowledgement is first due to all my talented colleagues, and clients at Grey Advertising. Many of the photographers, filmmakers, and artists I have worked with provided inspiration and friendship.

Acknowledgement is also due to my mentors. I started my career as a copywriter at the small but highly successful creative agency of Fältman & Malmén. The art director and company founder, Gunnar Fältman, taught me everything I know about classical advertising. My studies began by poring over the books on Gunnar's shelves. This was the best possible university for a copywriter.

Christian Preisler became my management partner at Grey and taught me the business side of advertising as well as a great deal about leadership. Together we created one of the leading advertising agencies in Scandinavia.

My final mentor is Ulf Jonströmer. Ulf founded the leading wireless technology consultancy Au-System and the incubator and venture capital company Brain Heart Capital. Ulf introduced me to the potential of Internet and wireless technology.

A number of well-known entrepreneurs have provided me with inspiration. These include Ingvar Kamprad of IKEA, Phil Knight of NIKE, and Body Shop's Anita Roddick. My real hero is Virgin's Richard Branson. As an aviator, I admire his ballooning adventures; as a branding consultant, I admire his example in using a brand to lead a business to success across a wide range of categories of products and services.

On the theoretical side, I am thankful for the work of Professor David Aaker, the branding guru, who was the first to recognize that a brand is a management tool, which can be used to drive an entire organization.

In the practical creation of this book I am indebted to Jan Lapidoth, my Swedish publisher at Bookhouse Publishing, and Richard Stagg of Financial Times/Prentice Hall. The business writers Stuart Crainer and Des Dearlove of Suntop Media provided editorial expertise.

Most of all, I am grateful for the support I receive from my family, and especially my partner in life Anette Rosencreutz, without whose spiritual support I would never have been able to bring this book to life.

Thomas Gad
London, December 2000

"It is better to believe than
to disbelieve, in so doing you
bring everything to
the realm of possibility"

Albert Einstein

THE METAPHOR
OF BRANDS

The brand as DNA

KNOWLEDGE IS A TOOL: not a privilege, not a right, not a monopoly. Knowledge needs to be put to use. I regard my knowledge about branding as software to be installed in my clients. My own role is to act as an installer, trainer, maintainer, and, sometimes, catalyst.

The 4-D Branding model explained in this book developed out of my work over many years. It is my own attempt to answer one important and often neglected question: How can companies futurize their brands? How can they create sustainable and robust brands that can act not just as window dressing, but as an engine to drive their businesses? The rise of the so-called Network Economy or New Economy makes that question more relevant – and more urgent. Finding an answer is the challenge that faces us all in the next few years.

What can I tell you about brands in the twenty-first century? The multitude of dot-com businesses currently competing for our attention confirms my view that brands will become more important than ever before. They are too important to be left to the marketing function – or any other single function, for that matter.

In search of inspiration, solutions to the branding challenges you now face, you may look up the profusion of books on the subject at Amazon.com. You probably won't find what you are looking for. Most books on brand management describe the success of established brands. They offer a retrospective rationale, or some idealized vision of the all-embracing brand position. But they don't provide the route map for getting to that destination. In particular, they offer no practical model for creating the brands of the future, especially Internet brands. Nor do they explain in any detail how companies can use their brand as a management tool to inform every aspect of the business.

The genetic programming that creates brands is something I call the Brand Code. In the Network Economy, the Brand Code equals business DNA. The Brand Code determines the characteristics of the business: what it looks like, how it feels, how it behaves. Not just *what* it is, but *who* it is – what makes it unique. The role of management is to establish the Brand Code – and to then use it to futurize the business.

I know these are bold claims. But think about it; the Network Economy is all about transparency. The Internet has accelerated a process that was already underway. Consumers have greater access to information than ever before. They are able to observe the internal workings of the companies they do business with. As they become more aware of their new power, they will peer into every nook and cranny. Transparent markets demand transparent organizations. Successful companies will be those that live the brand – because they are the brand.

To understand your brand fully, to live it and enable customers to live it, means creating your own Brand Code. To do so requires using a four-dimensional model to understand the strengths and weaknesses of your brand. The four dimensions are: functional, social, mental, and spiritual. (These are explained fully in Chapter 4.)

The functional dimension concerns the perception of benefit of the product or service associated with the brand.

The social dimension concerns the ability to create identification with a group.

The spiritual dimension is the perception of global or local responsibility.

The mental dimension is the ability to support the individual mentally.

If all the model afforded was a static view, a snapshot of the past or present, then its value would be limited. Instead, 4-D Branding offers a wind tunnel to test prototype brands against future scenarios, and this is what makes it so powerful. It is as a dynamic modelling tool that it is most valuable. It can just as easily be used to create a new brand as to analyze the strategic options for established brands.

By looking at brands in 4-D, organizations can create a Brand Code that can drive every aspect of the business – from product innovation to recruitment. Brand Code equals differentiation.

To be different is a biological drive. Naturally we seek to be different to avoid degeneration. Business life is nothing but an extension of other forms of life. In business, differentiation is equally important. If you're not different in business your whole existence is in danger. If you're not different you will be replaceable, and you will be under constant pressure to lower your price. Sometimes the only difference you need is not in the product you deliver, but in the way it is delivered.

Brand Mind Space™

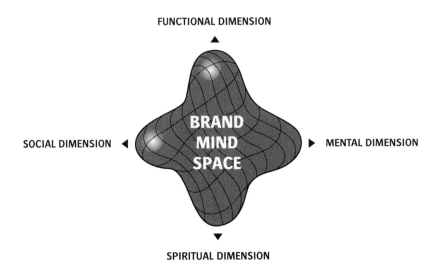

At the same time, sameness is also important. In a recent *Harvard Business Review* article, Kevin Keller, a professor at the Tuck School of Business, argues that a key attribute of successful brands is that they are properly positioned.[2] This involves understanding the importance of both competitive differences and parities. Parities are the areas of sameness. Keller's point is that by recognizing and building the points of parity, it is often possible to neutralize the competitive advantage of competing brands, while at the same time using points of difference to make your own brand distinctive.

He uses the example of the credit card company Visa to illustrate the point. In the 1970s, American Express differentiated its brand by appealing through the social status it conferred on card holders. It trumpeted the 'Membership has its privileges' message. In response, Visa introduced Gold and Platinum cards, and worked hard to raise the status of its brand. In doing so, it created a point of parity with American Express. At the same time, it also moved to extend its coverage so that it was accepted by many more stores and businesses. Convenience was its point of difference. The company created advertising featuring desirable, prestigious locations, with the message 'Visa. It's everywhere you want to be.' The brand offering successfully combined the point of parity and point of difference in one neat slogan. As a result, Visa took market share from American Express, not just in the family shopping market but in its rival's stronghold of international travel.

The Visa strategy worked because it created a point of parity, while offering a meaningful difference. To copy someone else's product or service exactly may work in the short term, but it will never be a brand, because a brand is a long-term differentiator.

Quite often business people feel disillusioned about providing difference in the product itself. I hear many statements along the lines of: 'There is really no difference, we all do the same.' This is not a good attitude. The right thinking is 'There is a possible difference, let's go out and find it.' Sometimes you have to go back through the history of your company to find the difference. Or you might try to see your difference by visioning your future.

The difference you are looking for might be very subtle, very hard for you to see. This is partly because you know exactly what your competitors are doing (and you rationalize all their efforts as more or less the same as what you are doing), but for a customer the difference you provide could possibly be of significant value. That's why it is sometimes good to be unaware of your competitors. Doing your own thing, without looking at what others are doing, can make you more genuinely different. Some of

Differentiation and Dramatization

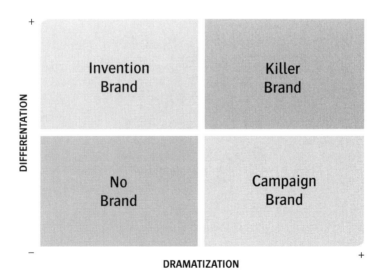

the examples of successful branding cases in this book are really about very small differences, mostly within the realm of beliefs. You have to start believing that there is a difference, otherwise no one else will believe it. It's a bit like making your hair stand up so you become taller.

Difference can always be found – if you look. Richard Branson introduced a guest book and massage on board Virgin Atlantic's jumbos because of his passion for differentiation. It was similar when Orange, the British mobile telecom operator, started charging per second instead of per minute, as was the tradition. In these details the brand becomes real.

Look and listen. Nike introduced a new tone to the world of advertising by telling its customers 'Just do it.' This was a totally different voice and provided much longer lasting differentiation than a detail in the construction of a shoe.

Differentiation can be found throughout any organization – supplier policy, product development, design, communication, sales, distribution, delivery, service, complaints, education, human resource management, investor relations, etc. But discovering difference first requires knowledge of the basic dynamics at work in 4-D Branding.

Nike Brand Mind Space

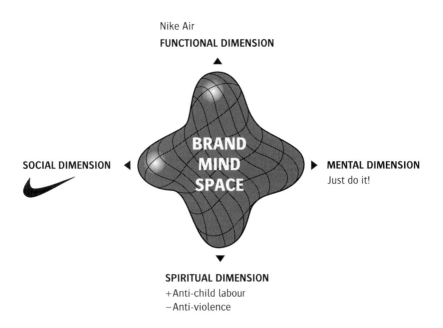

The basics of branding

TO ENABLE YOU to master the methods and models of 4-D Branding, you need to have some basic knowledge and insights about branding generally. Let's get back to basics. (If you feel you don't need this grounding, skip to page 23.)

The history of the word 'brand' goes back a long way. It started as a noun, but has gradually become a verb. To brand something is to make it more valuable. Branding adds value. That has always been the point of branding, and it is more true than ever whether you are branding a product, service, company, yourself, an event, or your art.

As a Scandinavian, I feel some pride in the fact that the word brand is supposedly Nordic in origin. At the time of the Vikings, branding meant marking cattle; more or less like today's trademark, a symbol of ownership, a guarantee of sorts. In modern business vocabulary, the distinction between 'trademark' and 'brand' is important and illustrative. (Even so, many senior managers honestly believe that a trademark is the same as a brand.) A 'trademark' can be registered and owned by a company, or a private person, over a lifetime. It's relatively easy to control its consequent use. Some companies even have a system of internal penalties for misuse of the trademark.

The level of recognition of a trademark can be built up in a very mechanical way. Sign the checks for banner ads, TV spots, and poster sites, and watch your exposure grow. The success of a trademark is largely measured by levels of awareness. (This can be calculated in customer research by prompted exposure with both symbol and logo, and non-prompted exposure using only the symbol.)

The Nike swoosh, for example, is a dream trademark. The symbol is recognized equally well with or without the word Nike. Remove the name and the swoosh still communicates which company is behind it. In 1971, the company paid $35 to art student Carolyn Davidson to come up with something quick that could be stitched on its sports shoes. It takes talent and skill – as well as some luck – to find such an ingenious form that is easily recognized by millions of pairs of eyes.

If creating a great brand were just about how much is spent on trademarks, then every big company would be a branding star. Money alone does not give a brand identity, still less personality. You have to know what it is that your brand stands for. Finding a compelling image requires a clear idea of the brand's essence. Take Virgin. 'When Virgin Records became successful we followed our instincts,' Richard Branson has observed. 'Initially the music reflected the "hippy" era and our logo of a naked lady back to back reflected that too. Then when Punk came along we felt we needed a crisper image... Rather than spending a fortune coming up with the new image, I was talking to our graphic designer one day explaining what we wanted and he threw on the floor his doodling – the now famous Virgin signature – which I fortunately picked up on the way to the loo.'

Trademarks, logos, badges – whatever you care to call them – have their place. But brands are more powerful and important than mere trademarks. Such is their power that you can change trademarks quite easily if you have a strong brand. (It sounds the height of folly to change a well-known trademark, but this is increasingly common and necessary thanks to the profusion of mergers, acquisitions, and sell-offs.)

Brands may be important, but they can't be registered and they can't be controlled – no matter how big and detailed a manual you produce. Nor can a brand be restricted to a single location. They defy geographic categorization and limitation. They do so because brands exist not in physical space but in people's minds, where the brand has left its mental footprint.

Footprints can be difficult to track. It may be a vague association of the time and place where the trademark was seen. Or a brand may be heavily imprinted as profound and intimate emotions. It may evoke a sense of a deep connection to the brand, based on cultural values or personal experiences that this trademark represents. And behind the latter can lie years of experience of the company or product.

In the past, the reputation of a tradesperson and the goodwill of a satisfied customer fulfiled much the same role as what we now call a brand. In medieval times in the Vatican, two forms of intellectual property were identified. One was the product itself and its design, the other was the reputation of the person making or selling the product. As a result, the Vatican had two courts to deal with intellectual property conflicts. For the first type, the trademark issues, the court consisted of secular lawyers who determined who had the rights to a particular trademark. The other court was part of the Church itself, handling the cases of reputation. To slander someone's business reputation was regarded as a sin.

The Vatican was right in recognizing that intangible assets, like image and reputation, have a value. In Europe we still treat goodwill as an asset on the balance sheet. This explains why brand valuation was born in Europe and not in the United States. To ignore the worth of such intangible assets remains a sin, to my eyes at least (if not the Pope's).

Why branding?

ALL THIS, OF COURSE, is abstract. The practically minded might ask whether, if the brand exists only in people's minds, it is at all meaningful or useful to try to control it. When every individual has, by definition, a totally different relationship with a brand, isn't it pointless to work on creating one image or positioning in the minds of all these individuals? Is establishing a single, congruent brand in everyone's mind simply an impossible dream?

The answer is no, it is not a dream – as countless branding successes can testify. But creating it is hard work.

If you have any doubts, consider the potency of branding. At root a nation is a brand, with the flag as the trademark and the national cultural values as the brand. People are still prepared to go to war, risking their lives for their nation and for those values.

Emile Durkheim in *Elementary Forms of The Religious Life* explains the religion of the Australian Aborigines. The concept of a church as Durkheim defines it is 'a shared feeling of a special kind.' It is group dynamics, the act of assembling for a common purpose, that creates the feeling of being in the presence of a spirit greater than the individual, a sacred feeling that strikes a chord with our deepest longings. Brands, too, strike chords.

However, striking the right chord is both difficult and often costly. There are no guarantees of the result, although there is a clear difference in the growth of financial value if you compare companies that have done at least a little branding and those that haven't branded themselves at all.

But what are the actual drivers influencing a company to invest in branding as a part of its strategy? The following are the most important.

The price driver

The market winner is usually the brand with the most coherent positioning in people's minds. This does not mean that everyone thinks of the brand in exactly the same way. That would be impossible, the way people think is unique to them. But if they think in similar enough ways, if there is sufficient overlap in their perceptions, a brand gains a feeling of coherence. It hangs together.

If this is achieved, the strangest things can happen. The most coherent brand is often preferred by many more customers than a less coherent competitor – even if the competitor is actually a better product or service. It may again be heresy, but this is a fact of commercial life. Consumers do not always choose the best. Tests have shown that simply telling people that a product, say a breakfast cereal, is made by a well-known company can make it seem to taste better than one made by a less well-regarded competitor. Consequently, the more coherent brand may also be able to charge more. Competitors may shake their heads at the paradox; a product that's not as good can be more expensive, and still have a larger market, than the better, cheaper product. Such is the magic of brands.

The corollary, of course, is that if customers are more satisfied with the branded product because they perceive it to be better, then they are getting value for money. The value added comes from their personal associations. (This is the mental dimension of our 4-D model, described later.)

The classic reason for building a brand is its ability to produce a higher margin. In marketing jargon we call this the *price premium*.

The idea sounds simple, but when it succeeds it is always impressive. Think of Intel – for the present at least, it is able to make the end customer pay 40 per cent more for a computer with an Intel processor than they would pay for the 18 or so other brands of microprocessors, whose technology is the equal of Intel's, sometimes even better. Branding works even in an extremely research-intensive high-tech business where engineering rules and there is no tradition whatsoever of branding or sophisticated marketing. You can imagine how hard it must have been to convince people at Intel that spending a fortune on the 'Intel Inside' branding strategy was a good idea. You can hear the skeptics, 'People don't give a damn what's inside their computer – they don't even know how to operate it on the outside!' Hands up now who thinks the cost of the branding initiative was money wasted? No one.

Intel: Putting a brand on chips

From a branding perspective, the Intel story is instructive for a number of reasons. The company was founded in 1968, when Gordon Moore and Robert Noyce left Fairchild Semiconductor to establish their own company. The rest is a whirlwind of technological history and huge commercial success. They were joined in their adventure by employee number four, Andy Grove, who became the company's celebrated CEO.

In 1971, Intel introduced the world's first microprocessor, the 4004. It also invented the high-speed memory (D-Ram) used in every kind of computer system. Such was its success that Intel had 10,000 employees by 1977. In the 1980s, Intel shrewdly refused to give other manufacturers a license to make its most powerful chips, so it made them all. In 1981, an

IBM PC based on the Intel microprocessor was launched, which helped sales reach $1 billion for the first time in 1984. A blip in 1986 saw Intel record a loss for the first time, but it speedily returned to profit in 1987 and in 1990 racked up its first $1 billion quarter, quickly followed, three years later, by its first $2 billion quarter.

For most of this time, Intel was unbranded and largely anonymous. Only Silicon Valley insiders and computer enthusiasts were really interested in where the chips come from. Even though it already held over 80 per cent of the PC-chip market, Intel decided that it wanted to become a known brand as well as hugely successful. It wanted everyone to be aware what was inside computers, doing the real work. The result was its Intel Inside campaign, which was hugely expensive – and very successful. People are now aware that Intel makes chips.

From nowhere, Intel became a top-ranking brand. By 1993 it was voted the world's third most valuable brand by *Financial World* magazine. Valued at $17.8 billion (compared to the worth of its nearest competitor at $4.1 billion), Intel lagged only behind Marlboro and Coca-Cola – quite an achievement.

Intel followed up its initial campaign with one for its Pentium chip. The logic behind this was that the Pentium was the newest and most powerful PC chip on the market. The Pentium was Intel's successor to the highly successful 266, 386, and 486 chips. After its launch at the beginning of 1994, Intel anticipated that sales of the Pentium would reach in excess of 10 million units by 1996. The campaign encouraged people to switch from 486 machines to Pentium PCs. All very laudable although, as Intel made the 486 chips, the company was waging war against itself. The campaign worked – it increased awareness of the Pentium – and also succeeded in annoying companies, such as Compaq, that were still putting their efforts into selling 486s. Compaq's marketing needed to find ways round the suggestion from the chip maker that the 486 was, basically, obsolete.

So far so good. Intel had become a branding triumph – proving that even something as seemingly dull as a computer microprocessor can become a consumer brand. But branding also has its more slippery side. Having revealed to the world that it makes the chips, Intel's troubles begin if the chips go wrong. It may be three million transistors on a tiny bit of silicon, but we expect it to be perfect and, thanks to Intel's marketing, if there is a fault in the chip we now know who to blame. Forget Dell or IBM, customers blame Intel.

'With Intel Inside you know you've got ... unparalleled quality,' read an Intel advertisement. The 'unparalleled quality' boast appeared a little excessive late in 1994 when Thomas Nicely, a mathematics professor at

Lynchburg College, Virginia, achieved international renown. Professor Nicely found that his three Pentium computers were making mistakes and then, in an effort to get to the bottom of the mystery, shared his discovery on the Internet. Thanks to the miracles of modern technology, a minor mathematical problem became an international incident. And, thanks to Intel's advertising, people knew where the fault lay. Once you create a brand, you have to take the flak if something goes wrong.

Whatever the nature and regularity of the flaw, Intel clearly had set itself up. Ironically, the problem with the Pentium was far less significant than flaws found in previous chips – the only difference was that Intel had marketed the brand too successfully. Not only had five million Pentiums been manufactured, but the Pentium was backed by an $80 million marketing campaign to encourage the market to make the switch from the old (the 486) to the new (the Pentium). This came on top of the estimated $70 million spent on the Intel Inside campaigns.

Intel's problems were largely of its own making. It created the brand and had to live with the consequences. Also, it was clearly a victim of its own success. The bigger the name, the bigger the brand, the keener competitors, onlookers, commentators, and journalists are to topple it from its pedestal. If you create a brand in one dimension as Intel did (the functional dimension), then you're in big trouble if you hit problems in that dimension.

Intel is just one story. There are many more examples of how branding has transformed an industry – or even created a new market. In many of these stories, the lead player has been able to charge a premium price for its brand initiative. Häagen-Dazs is able to get a 20 per cent higher price than its competitors in the premium ice-cream market. It was one of the super brands of the 1980s. This was a time of niche products and luxury brands. The indulgent ice-cream fitted the times perfectly. The advertisers added another ingredient that made it unstoppable – sex. The slogan 'dedicated to pleasure' and variations rapidly gave the dreamy ice-cream superstar status.

Few brands in recent years have used marketing as effectively as this US ice-cream producer. First, there was the exotic name, plucked from nowhere to add a Danish twist. Second came the carefully communicated brand promise – pure indulgence. Only the finest ingredients were used to produce what was always positioned as a luxury consumer product. Häagen-Dazs broke the rules by transforming a children's treat into a luxury indulgence for adults.

The ice-cream brand always commanded a premium price, but somehow, far from putting consumers off, it seemed to appeal to their desire for self-indulgence. Everything about the brand, from its sensual advertising to its packaging, invited consumers to spoil themselves. Here was the ultimate in hedonistic pleasure; sex and ice-cream, together. It didn't get any better than this. No matter that they couldn't afford the best of everything, in one area of their lives they could go all the way. Millions did just that.

Time magazine described Häagen-Dazs as 'the best ice-cream in the world.' The brand virtually invented the premium ice-cream market. Others soon followed, but, at the moment, Häagen-Dazs is still ahead. Market research shows it to be the clear brand leader (except for own-label brands).

We attach different values to anything that has to do with taste or style. In a blind test it is almost impossible to taste the difference between Häagen-Dazs and other, cheaper, premium ice-creams. That's a fact. When I mention this in my seminars there is always someone in the audience who protests. They defend their favourite ice-cream brand in front of everyone else. They care about it even if the rest of the audience does not.

Brands can have that effect. Strong brands can create a friendship-like relationship between the brand and the consumer (see the later section on the brand as a friend). People are loyal to their friends, and will often forgive their faults.

You might think that the logic of paying a premium price for a good brand has always existed. Not so. At the end of the 1980s and the beginning of the 1990s, a wave of mistrust about the value of brands swept through a variety of markets, particularly in the United States, the home of the commercial brand. Private labels and powerful distributors squeezed their suppliers, brand values were deflated, and suppliers responded with very shortsighted attempts to 'buy' customers with coupons and discounts. Consumers proudly declared their independence from the lure of 'name brands' in favour of the practicality of generic products. Then came Marlboro Friday, when the cigarette maker dramatically lowered its prices. (Interestingly, on the same day the brands on the stock market also went down, showing that at least the financial market believed in brands.)

Today, faith in brands has totally recovered. The 1997 Yankelovich Monitor survey of American consumers shows that a known/trusted brand name is a strong influence on purchase decisions for 63 per cent of respondents, up from 51 per cent in 1994. No wonder the trend is upward. The average consumer sees 1500 ads a day; the average store has 25,000 different products on its shelves. With so much noise in the marketplace, we're all glad to see old friends among the crowd.

The volume driver

Another reason to work with brands – also obvious, but nevertheless important – is the *volume premium*. It is a simple fact that a well-known brand that also stands for something special and good usually creates a larger audience and market than a less well-known brand.

Some brands are conceived as volume brands from the start. Often they have a low price. To get this low price you usually have to give up something: convenience, service, or something else. At H&M clothing stores you may value the trendiness of the fashionwear, rather than the quality of the cloth or how well it fits you.

IKEA: The flatpack brand

One of the finest exponents of the volume brand is IKEA. The Swedish furniture company is a truly great retail brand. It has endeared itself to younger, price-conscious homemakers in the 39 countries in which it operates. To them, IKEA – with its DIY assembly from flatpacks – represents stylish design at affordable prices. To the loyal customers who fill its stores, IKEA is self-assemble chic.

IKEA FACTS & FIGURES

Turnover (1998-99) $8.48 billion

IKEA has 2,330 suppliers in 64 countries.

49,000 co-workers – compared with 15 in 1954; 250 in 1964; 1,500 in 1974; 8300 in 1984; and 26,600 in 1994.

Rising from its humble origins in Småland, a rural area of Sweden, IKEA has grown from a tiny mail-order business to a $5.8 billion furniture giant with more than 140 stores and 39,000 employees. The brand is driven by the, sometimes quirky, philosophies of its founder Ingvar Kamprad. The company name bears the initials of the farm and his home community – I(ngvar) K(amprad) E(lmtaryd = the farm) A(gunnaryd = the community).

IKEA Brand Mind Space

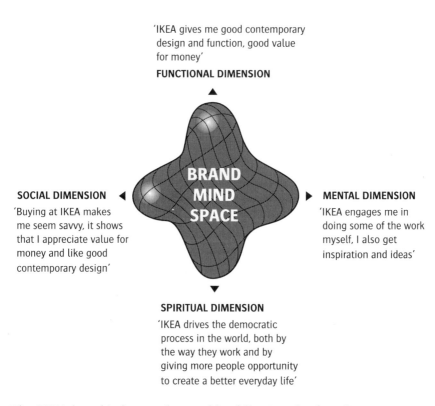

'IKEA gives me good contemporary design and function, good value for money'

FUNCTIONAL DIMENSION

SOCIAL DIMENSION
'Buying at IKEA makes me seem savvy, it shows that I appreciate value for money and like good contemporary design'

BRAND MIND SPACE

MENTAL DIMENSION
'IKEA engages me in doing some of the work myself, I also get inspiration and ideas'

SPIRITUAL DIMENSION
'IKEA drives the democratic process in the world, both by the way they work and by giving more people opportunity to create a better everyday life'

The IKEA brand is best understood by following the four dimensions framework:

FUNCTIONAL

IKEA aims to give customers good quality, highly practical, contemporary design at affordable prices. IKEA's mission statement distils its functional objectives: 'To contribute to a better everyday working life for the majority of people, by offering a wide range of home furnishing items of good design and function, at prices so low that the majority of people can afford to buy them.'

Low prices and cost efficiency are the driving forces of the IKEA brand. They stem directly from the personality of Ingvar Kamprad and the corporate culture he has created. IKEA's culture is based on the values of Småland, where Kamprad grew up. The inhabitants of this part of Sweden are renowned for being cost-conscious, hard-working and creative.

Kamprad is famously very down to earth. Even in his seventies, he visits 20 stores every year. For each he writes a report. Walking around he continually asks whether products offer value for money. His constant question is 'How much would you pay for this?' Kamprad is a master of symbolic actions. When he visits a store he always checks the garbage container and nearly always finds something that someone has thrown away, but he thinks should have been sold off cheaply. It is even suggested that he sometimes asks for something to be put in the garbage so he can make his point.

The result is that IKEA has 20–30 per cent lower prices than its competitors. Yet, somehow IKEA continues to squeeze increasing returns from its retail units: it has been estimated that IKEA's sales per square metre are twice the industry's average.

Low cost is combined with a strong emphasis on functionality. Its designs are basic, undemonstrative, unfussy. A simple, white-lacquered bookshelf called Billy has been selling well for 20 years. Such lucrative simplicity is testimony to the fact that IKEA knows its customers' minds. Its product development process emphasizes practical detail – such as what's the bathroom like at seven o'clock in the morning in a family with four children. What are their needs? How should things function?

This attention to detail mean that IKEA is also willing to change quickly if products aren't selling. In recent years, it has succeeded where many European retailers have failed, successfully taking its formula to North America. This experience was not without its lessons. Puzzled at first by poor sale of beds and other lines, IKEA quickly learned that although Americans liked the simplicity of its designs, they wanted furniture to match their larger homes. The answer? Bigger furniture. IKEA also discovered that in the US most families have several TV units at home; this led it to start making TV furniture.

SOCIAL

The perception of customers is that buying at IKEA gives them a sound profile. It shows that they appreciate value for money and like good contemporary design.

Interestingly, IKEA's home-spun philosophy combining the virtues of simplicity and making do with a commitment to equality and innovation appears in step with modern times. The company was one of the first to use recycled materials in furniture, for example, although this was more out of a desire to keep down costs than to be seen as 'green.' Being financially attractive and environmentally responsible is a double whammy most brands struggle to pull off – IKEA did so almost accidentally.

MENTAL

Customers feel good when buying from IKEA because they feel they have used their money well and got very good value for money. They also feel they have been inspired and received many new ideas as to what they would like to do with their home in the future. There is also the instant gratification of taking home the product immediately rather than waiting for it to be delivered.

IKEA seeks to make shopping easy, entertaining and informative. Its strategy is to build outside cities so that it can benefit from good road infrastructures and lower land prices. This potato field strategy means that its stores are easy to get to and have lots of free parking space.

The IKEA store situated south of Stockholm is one of the largest tourist attractions in Sweden, with more than 3 million visitors a year. According to one senior executive at the company's headquarters in the Swedish town of Almhult: 'The only way of keeping the customer long-term in our vision is that he has a benefit from coming to IKEA. The product and price quality that we offer must be the best. We even say that we must have better prices than our competitors as one of our operating principles. That is basic to our long-term success.

'From there, we say, how can we make a visit to IKEA a day out. IKEA should be a day out. That started in the first store here in Almhult. In the old days to come to our store they had to leave early in the morning. The journey would usually take a couple of hours and many of our customers had small children.' Hence the family restaurants and crèche facilities that have become a feature of IKEA stores (on weekends and holidays, the company even employs clowns and magicians to entertain the kids).

The logic is pragmatic. 'We believe that the prices in our restaurants should be very good so that customers with young families can afford to eat there and not have to bring sandwiches. They shouldn't have to leave IKEA just because they are hungry.'

SPIRITUAL

IKEA pronounces its aim is 'To create a better everyday life for the majority of people.' It sees itself as part of the democratization process. This may have helped its international development. Few retail businesses has been able to succeed on an international level, IKEA belongs to these few who have most of their sales outside their home country, others are Benetton, Body Shop and H&M. It has positioned itself as a universal company selling products with universal benefits.

IKEA's argument is that the company works in a democratic way and gives more people opportunities to create a better everyday life through fairly-priced home furnishings.

The spiritual element is internally very strong. The IKEA culture is based around simple beliefs but ones that are strongly held. Kamprad has called these the nine commandments – they include 'simplicity is a virtue' and 'profit gives us resources.' An engaged staff is crucial. The company always uses the term 'co-workers' rather than employees. Kamprad embodies the business idea and the corporate culture. His extensive and frequent visits to stores have an invaluable impact on the corporate culture.

The result is that IKEA is one the most culture-driven companies in the world. It skillfully uses corporate culture as a management tool to maintain a feeling of togetherness. The corporate culture and values are communicated within, as well as outside, the company by way of clear symbols and symbolic actions. (On every folder or printed matter used by the company its value is printed. This reminds people of the fact that everything has a cost.) Important words, such as cost consciousness, simplicity and enthusiasm, are continually emphasized.

The IKEA brand is an unusual – perhaps unique – concord between the business idea, the range of products, the corporate culture and the leadership. Such potent combinations are hard-won and, for mere mortals, highly elusive. Few have Kamprad's attention to detail or uncanny ability to know the marketplace. The challenge for IKEA and its new CEO, Anders Dalvik, is to sustain its brand strength without Kamprad and in the face of mounting competition from companies including Pricesclub, Wal-Mart, MFI and Conforma.

1926 Ingvar Kamprad born
1946 First advertisement for IKEA
1950 Furniture introduced at IKEA
1951 First IKEA catalogue
1955 IKEA start designing its own furniture
1956 Launches flat parcels containing 'put-it-together-yourself-furniture'
1965 First store in Stockholm, launch of self-service (the customers pick up the goods at the warehouse themselves)
1976 Ingvar Kamprad writes 'The testament of a furniture dealer'

Vaccinating against disaster

IN EVERY BUSINESS things can go wrong, and usually will do so at some point. It can lead to a total catastrophe. Think back to when Perrier's mineral water was found to be contaminated and the company had to withdraw every bottle from the shelf. This allowed its competitors, Italian and other foreign waters, to take Perrier's place. Nevertheless, the strength of the Perrier brand enabled it to bounce back, despite the business being severely damaged.

Another example of a truly remarkable recovery is that of Mercedes-Benz and its small A-class car. A Swedish car journalist did the usual 'elk-test,' a manoeuver on a test range in which the car is put though a series of sharp and sudden turns to prove it can cope if a large obstacle (such as an elk) suddenly appeared in the road. The Mercedes A-class didn't handle well at all; to everyone's surprise, including the journalist, the car rolled over, ending up on its roof. The picture of the event spread quickly and the A-class appeared to be stillborn.

Thanks to its very strong brand – on a functional, as well as a social dimension – Mercedes had a second chance. It put all of its engineering efforts into making the car safe. It was retested, and passed with flying colours. But without the strong Mercedes brand and its association with safety and reliability, the A-class car would have completely disappeared from the market. Imagine if it had been produced by a less prestigious manufacturer or had been a new brand; it would not have survived to tell the tale. The strength of the brand not only allowed the product to recover, it helped make the A-class into one of the trendiest cars in Europe. A year-and-a-half after the catastrophe, Mercedes was quoting a six-month delivery time. The elk test failure had been transformed from a corporate disaster into a triumph of Mercedes engineering.

Contrast the A-class recovery with what happened when Skoda went through the same experience. Its car also rolled in a test. As a consequence, the brand practically vanished from the Western market – until over 10 years later when Volkswagen, with its brand power and trustworthiness, brought it back to the international market.

I call the amazing recovery power of a good brand the *vaccination* effect. All you invest in your brand and what it stands for is like a vaccination. This life insurance policy is worth every penny in the payback you will get from a fast recovery in the market if, and when, your business becomes infected. A stronger brand also has a better chance of surviving a dip in the economy, while weaker brands will suffer severely. The number one brand in each market segment will always come out of an ailing economy better, and with a chance of recovering faster than the market recovers, than a number two, three, or four brand in the same segment.

The financial value

IN RECENT YEARS, the strongest motivation for investing in a brand has simply been the effect it has on the *financial value* of the company that owns the brand. The basis for this brand value is usually called *brand equity*, a recognized bottom-line value distinct from product sales revenues. A brand's equity is the added value that allows it to charge a higher price for its product than the less well-known alternative. The brand equities of companies like Coca-Cola, Microsoft, IBM and Intel are valued in billions of dollars. Every well-known brand possesses a brand equity.

Brands are now commonly regarded as investments. The stock market is a market of brands, and this is clearly shown in a chart showing share prices on the London stock exchange. Strongly branded companies simply perform better than those professing not to care about branding. This is likely to become ever more true. The more public the markets become, the more important it will be to be a brand – a good brand, a brand with a future.[3]

In the past, a strong brand brought with it a solid and stable market, and healthy revenues. This will always be fundamental, but now well-known brands, such as Nokia, are exceptionally highly appreciated, with higher share prices than those for other brands in the same business.

A small number of corporations attempt to calculate the value of their brands in their annual reports. At the moment, the financial value of a brand is seldom exposed until it (or the owning company) is bought or sold. This might change in the future.

There are many ways to value a brand and later I will explain a means of brand valuation linked to my methods of brand building. However, for a very rough idea of the value of a brand without access to all the inside data otherwise required, look at the market price of the company, its market capitalization (the sum of all shares at present market quotation). From that, subtract the net assets of the company, its book value (this information is in the annual report). The difference is the excess value of the company as decided by the market.

This difference in value may contain many things that do not entirely depend on the brand itself. These may include patents, long-term contracts

Branding Increases the Stockmarket Value

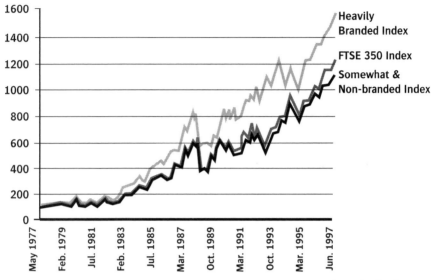

Source: Interbrand

with customers, or speculation about opportunities in the market due to changes in legislation, etc. Very roughly, you can take 50 per cent from the excess value to account for everything that is not related to the brand. The remaining 50 per cent is the very rough value of the brand.

If you do this operation on the values in the chart above, based on the *Financial Times* index of the 100 largest corporations in the UK, you will see that amazing values are now tied to brands. Indeed, research shows that between 30 and 70 per cent of the market value of a company is related to its brand or brands – this is based on a selection of companies in different industries and businesses. Little wonder that brands are getting more attention than ever before.

Shorter lifecycles

IN A RAPIDLY changing world, the *lifecycle* of products and services is becoming ever shorter. The focus on the product that most businesses had just 10 years ago is now challenged by focus on the brand. Products come and go with ever-increasing rapidity, but the brand is here to stay.

Most of the classic brands evolved alongside a unique product. In such relationships, the brand and the product are impossible to separate. Today, however, many brands exist almost independently of their associated products.

Take fashion. Brands such as Calvin Klein and Versace are used to brand not only fashionwear, but also fragrances, eyewear, interior design, and even cars. Since product lifecycles are getting shorter, the range of products covered by the brand is getting wider, as most companies prefer concentrating on one or a very few master brands. Under this brand name they use more or less generic product codes, numbers or letters indicating a different product, but without creating new sub-brands challenging the master brand.

When you do this your master brand becomes more valuable, but also more sensitive. You are effectively putting all your eggs in one basket. Such a branding strategy requires branding to be a core part of corporate strategy. Half measures will end in failure.

Using the brand to propel the company

THE FINAL USE for a brand is as a *management tool*. Look at IKEA. Branding can exert a powerful influence over the way a company is run, how it does business, where it is, and where it is going. Using the brand as a management tool is one very powerful way to make your life as a business leader easier; a way to be truly on top of things, rather than a victim of circumstances.

A strong brand has a beneficial effect on your relationships with all the major stakeholders in your business:

EMPLOYEES

A strong brand, a well-defined brand with good core values, will enable you to have your pick of the best people from the universities or the job market, and they will work for you for lower salaries, fewer fringe benefits, while making fewer demands for personal development. It always amazes me how little some of the leading brands have to pay to get the best people. A brand like Virgin attracts bright young things like moths to a flame. This shows clearly that people don't work for money, they work for something to believe in, and for something to give them an identity. The unknown and the uncool hold little allure.

In their book, *Funky Business*, Kjell Nordström and Jonas Ridderstråle suggest that old economy *modus operandi* of hiring for skills and training for attitude needs now to be replaced with a belief in hiring for attitude and training for skill.

It makes obvious sense. If you are seated at dinner next to someone who is working for a company you have never heard of, or about which you know nothing, your interest in that person will be very limited. In contrast, if your neighbour works for IBM, McDonald's, British Airways, or Volkswagen, all of a sudden that person has an identity. Similarly, your personal value on the job market is often transformed when you are able to refer to a strong brand as your present or previous employer. Sometimes the branding effect in these cases is so strong, and we are so impressed, that we completely forget to evaluate what position such people actually have in that company, or what work they are doing.

The attraction of branding is plainly appreciated by the management consulting industry. Consulting firms only really discovered branding during the last decade. Key to this was a realization that a strong brand attracts the brightest brains. Such is the lure of the dot-com world that even the major management consulting firms are finding it tough to recruit their quota of bright young things. At the same time, hypercompetition between the consulting giants means that differentiation is vital. Brand recognition is all important. Branding has become a competitive arena for these firms. One estimate puts the amount spent by each of the leading consulting firms on brand-boosting ads as $50 million or more. Interestingly, much of it is not aimed directly at clients.

Consulting firms discovered advertising in 1989 when Andersen Consulting split from Arthur Andersen. The new consulting firm's early ads asked if we remembered the geek in the class who was good at calculus. They went on to say that the geek now worked for Andersen. The ads keep coming – a single issue of one business magazine included 14 colour ads from Andersen.

These ads are taking firms in surprising new directions. 'Not everyone can wait ten years for a new drug to come to market,' reads a three-page spread from PricewaterhouseCoopers featuring a portrait of a man from an underdeveloped country who has just been inoculated. It ends with the punchline: 'We're helping make sure they don't have to. Join us. Together we can change the world.' Remember, all this money and all these bright campaigns are being targeted at talented people rather than potential customers.

OWNERS

Shortsighted shareholders, private or public, can be magically patient if your brand building promises a future cash-in situation, be it a takeover, merger, or just a very strong position on the stock market. Branding is in itself, as we have seen, usually a good way to make a company more attractive to financial analysts. Just ask Jeff Bezos, founder of Amazon.com. Amid all the hullabaloo, Amazon's stock market value has remained high despite recent problems in the sector and increasing losses.

PUBLIC OPINION

Last, but not least, a strong brand offers a good platform for handling public opinion. Of course, you will be more of a target if something goes wrong, as Intel discovered, but remember the vaccination effect. The positive benefits of being a well-known, good, open, and positive brand are truly enormous. Your competitors will be in agony at the amount of press and attention you routinely receive – sometimes well out of proportion to your news value or performance. Life is so unjust; stronger brands become even stronger, with help from the media.

This explains why in so many markets the distance between brand number one and brand number two is so enormous. If your company becomes a brand leader, it will jump on an escalator that is moving exponentially upward, and it will be very hard, perhaps even impossible, for competitors to catch up.

I like to see the effect of a strong and good brand as the hub on a propeller; every blade of the propeller helps to power the company, the blades being customers, employees, owners, and public opinion, the company's primary stakeholder groups. The hub keeps the propeller together while moving it ceaselessly forward.

"If you think that you are too small
to have an impact, try going
to bed with a mosquito in the room"

Anita Roddick, founder of Body Shop

NEW
REALITIES

Branding in the Network Economy

THE FUNDAMENTALS OF BRANDING are now being implemented and rein-
vented in a new world. As countless commentators have pointed out, the
world of business is undergoing substantial changes. Brands are not im-
mune to these changes. Indeed, in many cases they are leading the charge
towards change.

The new realities are all pervasive. Today's competitive environment
puts incredible pressure on business leaders. Companies often seem as if
they are being pulled apart by the different interests among their major
stakeholders.

And it is not only the market that is increasingly demanding. Customers
require that companies give them full attention. They like to be treated
like friends, but making friends with them has never been more complex.
Customers now have more alternatives, greater control, and are becoming
more competent and better informed. There is also a profusion of new competitors in most businesses. By using new information technology, they
can appear on the worldwide market from nowhere. Five years ago, who
had heard of Amazon.com?

The flip side is that in five years' time, many of today's New Economy
stars will be no more than a distant memory. Like one-hit wonders, they
are pervasive today, but could slip back into obscurity with startling ease.
Picking losers is an even more dangerous game than picking winners. It is
impossible to know which of the new arrivals will successfully futurize
their brands. It's not about which of the dot-coms is making the most noise
now, it's about which is creating a brand for tomorrow and beyond.

The challenge facing managers is intense. Whether you work in New or
Old Economy companies, the expectations are unparalleled: greater competition, more demanding customers and, on top of all that, hugely demanding employees. Recent research shows that for young business people
personal freedom and development are more important than regular compensation. They believe that working hard and with commitment will
bring its own benefits. Better to learn than to earn.

The fast-growing IT companies set a new standard for these young
executives. Everyone wants to work in an exciting dot-com business. The

turn-on is not (only) the pot of gold, but the sheer buzz of being in the right place at a happening time.

High expectations mean that in many business areas it is increasingly difficult to recruit the best people – as we have seen in the consulting business. The most competent and skilled people ask for more than just being paid well. This is especially true among the youngest employees, who expect personal development as a right and believe that work is supposed to be challenging rather than secure. This means that companies have to offer everything from sophisticated job rotation to very specialized education. None of this is cheap. If you want the best people, it will usually cost you a lot.

There is more. Competitors, customers, and employees are supplemented by demanding owners. The owners of your company might be a private group of people, easy to communicate with. But in many companies professional investors have seats on the board, and they will certainly be there if you are a public company. In all cases, the question is how to meet the demand for short-term profit, and this issue will take up much of your attention – attention and energy that should be spent on the company's long-term development.

Finally, there is the most fickle corporate force of all – public opinion. Suddenly, journalists, business opinion leaders, environmentalists, lawyers, and others appear from nowhere, driven by potential publicity, looking for a case to make.

In turbulent seas the use and power of your propeller is liable to be questioned. A great many established business people still think that the New Economy is a sea of dreams. 'What's wrong with the old economy?' they ask. The old economy is fine; it does a job. But it won't be able to do it in the same way in the future.

The Network Economy changes the rules. Information-powered by the Internet, the new network economy will dramatically change the relationships and assumptions underpinning traditional industrial businesses. Pumped up by high-speed communication technology, the New Economy is characterized by networking, globalization, transparency, rapid growth, flat organizations, and very young management.

Despite the current hype, I believe that the change will be gradual, but nevertheless rapid. My message is not aimed at the dot-com shooting stars of today, but at the entrepreneurs who want to secure a place in the business constellation of tomorrow. When the speculative frenzy has turned into a more serious debate, some of the current crop of dot-coms will remain. They will be the ones who understand the power of branding.

For e-commerce operations the brand is not only important to safeguard on-line monetary transactions, it is necessary for stimulating the customer-initiated pull marketing on which the efficiency of commerce on the Web is built. But the brand is also vital to ensure quality, and to assist customers in handling the information overload on the Web.

The case of AltaVista versus Yahoo! is interesting and educational. Savvy Internet users praise AltaVista for its search engine's superior qualities, but its former parent Digital Equipment Corp and later Compaq didn't follow up with sufficient marketing. Yahoo! became quickly dominant and AltaVista languished. But that was not the whole truth.

Founded in 1994 by David Filo and Jerry Yang, two Stanford electrical engineering students, Yahoo! started as a hobby when Filo and Yang decided to find a better way of keeping track of their personal interests on the Internet. The result was a hierarchical index – or Yet Another Hierarchical Officious Oracle (YAHOO) – they then set out to improve it.

Once it was posted up on the net, with a search facility to allow specific sites to be found, surfers flocked to use it. At the start Yahoo! lived on the Stanford University system with the Yahoo! index on Yang's workstation and the search engine on Filo's PC. Fortunately for the efficiency of the Stanford network, Marc Andreessen, then at Netscape, suggested they moved their files over to some Netscape machine. Even better, Netscape didn't charge them.

From there the business just took off. Yang and Filo struggled on by themselves for some time before taking on extra staff. Even when they were operating from Netscape premises and getting 2 million accesses a day there was just the two of them doing everything. Today, the company has offices in Europe, the Asian Pacific, Latin America, Canada and the US, with headquarters in Santa Clara, California.

Yahoo! stands for a totally different personality and for other values. The engineering-driven AltaVista promotes functional dimensions, whereas Yahoo! creates a community and a strong social dimension. Overall, it is a much more social brand. And it also shaped a strong mental dimension of a cool, good inner feeling, a true friend helping me out on the Net, versus the technological wizard and wise guy of AltaVista. Now the new owners of AltaVista will have to spend millions of dollars to get AltaVista back on the map, hopefully also creating a better brand personality.

What this demonstrates is that brands on the Web undergo the same basic rules as brands off the Web. They will need both a good Brand Code and marketing support, usually done outside the Web in traditional media channels, in order to make success long term.

Building context

DURING THE EARLIER STAGES of the Web, production and distribution technology dominated. The AltaVista model. There was total focus on the transaction service, the search engines and the e-mail communication. Understandably, this focus was usually provided by technologists.

The second stage in the Web's development was an emphasis on content, the substance of the service. This is all about packaging services to create differentiation. Look at the development of fatbrain.com which specializes in delivering one-stop digital publishing solutions to corporate clients, including 300 *Fortune 1000* companies. Fatbrain can facilitate the cataloguing, publishing and delivering of corporate documents all via the Internet.

In addition Fatbrain provides access to one of the largest selections of technical information in the world; books, training and certification courses, industry research, technical papers and business texts are all part of Fatbrain's extensive repertoire.

Digital Value Propositions

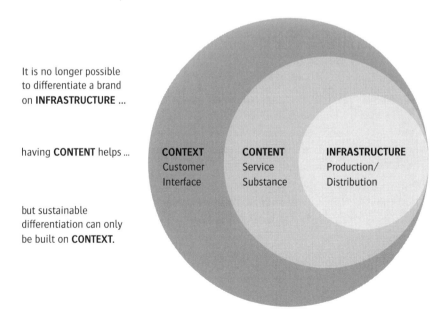

It is no longer possible to differentiate a brand on **INFRASTRUCTURE** ...

having **CONTENT** helps ...

but sustainable differentiation can only be built on **CONTEXT**.

CONTEXT
Customer
Interface

CONTENT
Service
Substance

INFRASTRUCTURE
Production/
Distribution

As well as supplying B2B services, Fatbrain also allow consumers to buy eMatter publications, delivered via their secure digital publishing technology. The eMatter channel incorporates new secure digital rights technologies and features original works by well-known authors such as science fiction writer Arthur C Clarke and Internet marketing guru Seth Godin. Fatbrain is a great example of the power of content in helping build a brand presence.

But there needs to be more. The final element in New Economy brand building is context; the consumer or customer interface that creates the relations and associations: pictorial language, attitudes and values. This is often the forgotten element.

In the Network Economy, building context is the route to long-term differentiation.

Building context first requires that you understand that on the Web you are transparent, easily compared with others, in direct contact with your end customer, or user, or member. You receive immediate response on every activity. You will be scrutinized. You will be asked questions and you are expected to socialize and entertain. There are no half measures. Testing something on the Web is always full scale. Even if you choose to do it in one country domain first, technically everybody can (and will) watch you. There is nowhere to hide.

In the traditional business, non-transparency was an efficient method of making money. Markets were kept apart by lack of information, different pricing policies were applied to different customer segments, different qualities were delivered in products under the same brand or sub-brand on different markets, products from one market could be dumped on another, and so on. No wonder the customer always had a suspicion of being fooled.

Now customers are empowered by information, of which the typical proof is the spread of auctions on the Web. An auction is by definition transparent as everybody has the same information throughout the auction process.

Transparency will be taken for granted by everybody from now on. Watch out – don't make the mistake of giving out different information to different groups of customers about the same product or offer. There is nothing more dangerous, more undermining of the trust in your brand.

You can embrace transparency in many ways. The most important is to be open with information about your products, their origins, ecological qualities, your ethics, etc. The Web is excellent for building a serious, and deeper, knowledge and understanding about your product. In classical advertising this would never have been possible; in brochures it would have been perceived as too heavy, or specialized. For customers who are concerned about responsibility (and these are a growing number), you can easily provide them with that information in great detail. (Take a look at the Nike site to find out how the company is now handling the question of child labour.)

Standing for something

CONTEXT ALSO REQUIRES that your brand has to stand for something. It has to create a philosophy. It must tell a story. It must resonate with authenticity. Remember the difference between AltaVista and Yahoo!.

Differentiation is always necessary in branding, but on the Web it's even more important. On the Web there is so much noise, so much clutter. It's so easy for anyone to get their business in, and so very hard for everybody to get their message out. To stand out is a nightmare. What's your recipe? What's your story? What's your philosophy?

Forget status; think philosophy. To have a *philosophy* is important to all business, but on the Web it's essential. Because of its transparency everything will be easy to compare on the Web. If you don't have time to do this comparing yourself, and most of us won't, then it will be done by professionals on the Web: journalists, organizations, brokers, and so on. There will be plenty of room for all kinds of information compilers on the Internet. That is why it's so important to have a philosophy. An outspoken business philosophy and a different business idea cannot be ignored, they demand to be commented on, usually as an add-on benefit, provided that the rest of the product packages compared are on a par.

Personality also serves as a differentiator. A website with a distinctive voice is instantly recognizable – and has the advantage that the cost of changing your message is low. Creating *value* has to do with customization, the ability to tailor a product or a service so perfectly to the needs of a customer, and in a way that will make the customer feel he or she is absolutely satisfied.

Exceeding customer expectations is the best way to produce a perception of value in that customer. This works even better if you can address values that you *know* are important to the customer. If you over-deliver using the cheaper *surprise* effect, rather than by giving more of the product for the money and thus lowering your margins, you might still do good business. In order to do this you have to be playful and creative. Again, you can now do this economically through the Web.

Charm has to do with the ability to be really personal, to address people individually. Thanks to the low cost of storing information about previous purchases and the individual interests of each customer, charm has never been cheaper.

To be *authentic* and to be a good storyteller will be of great value when you're branding on the Web. There will always be space for telling the real story of how you started your business and did what you did. The more personal and charming you can be the better. To be small is beautiful and to be personal is OK, because you are now communicating in a personal way directly to an individual. To be big and impressive was good when you were mass communicating, now it's not necessarily an advantage any more – being individual and intimate is more chic.

Building relationships

CONTEXT LEADS TO CONNECTIONS; connections that create relationships. There is an intimacy on the Web that is unique compared with traditional media. The idea is actually more important than the product. No medium has been more able to build *relationships* and create interactivity automatically and cheaply.

More and more relationships are being created. The customer of the future will demand true relationships more and more.

Relationships require *trust*. This is one of the most important factors in the success of e-commerce. Some of the difficulties that many Web shops now experience are probably, in part, to do with this. Buyers on the Net now are early adopters, the most daring customers, prone to experimentation and fond of trying out new things. The major market segments still remain to be won, but Web buyers will only arrive by trust and reference.

Brands are the route to establishing trust. The leading e-commerce companies excel in the number of confirmation messages you receive as a result of your purchase. It works. Jeff Bezos sends you an email from Amazon.com and you know it's an automatic mechanical thing, but it still impresses. References from other customers, such as the customer book reviews at Amazon.com, are now copied by every bookshop on the Web. Also the design has to appeal to people seeking trust. Familiar things will be more important than the latest Java technique.

The oldest role of the brand, as the guarantee of quality, will experience a renaissance. But in addition to that, to create trust the brand also has to add personality, charm, relation, and value. What is interesting is that over the Internet many of these things are easier to do in a more customized and cheaper way.

Creating customer communities

ONE RELATIONSHIP IS not enough. You need to build a profusion of relationships. Think about communities.

A *Which? Online* survey conducted in 1999 by Mori found that about 1 million over 55s, in the UK, were regularly using the Internet. And 32 per cent of these so-called silversurfers had purchased goods or services online compared to only 11 per cent of users in the 15 to 54 age group.

Vavo.com was set up by Richard Spinks to serve the online needs of silversurfers. The Vavo website offers more than simply tailored content for its target audience. It has an online shop offering products aimed specifically at the site's registered users. To ensure that its customers get what they want Vavo asks them first. For example, before offering a low-cost insurance package to its visitors, it quizzed them on their particular likes and dislikes regarding health insurance products in an online survey.

From the very start Vavo demonstrated its desire to understand exactly what silversurfers want from an online site. In an unusual move, Spinks appealed to the fifty-plus age group to help build the site through an advert placed in a magazine. And although it's a tough proposition offering content to satisfy such a disparate group of users Vavo has identified several common interest areas such as finance and health.

As the largest website of its type in the UK – over 50,000 registered members and 700,000 visits a month – and one of the first movers, Vavo is well positioned to ride the silversurfing wave.

Another company to figure the community ethic is Boots the Chemist, a stalwart of the British high street. It is a company that conjures up words like safe, traditional, solid. You would be forgiven for thinking it a sound business, if a little dull, but hardly at the forefront of Internet e-commerce. However, in this case you would be mistaken.

Handbag.com was launched in October 1999, a product of a collaboration between the Boots company and Hollinger Telegraph New Media. This 50/50 joint venture was the first UK Internet service designed exclusively for women. At the time of the launch research suggested that of the 8 million or so UK Internet users 40 per cent were women. A figure expected to rise to 2 million users by 2004, by which time 50 per cent of all users are expected to be women.

The site offers a variety of themed channels such as beauty, health, fashion, and news. Each has its own editor and experts on hand to offer advice to surfers who email their questions in. There is also free Internet access and email available to those who want it. And, of course, online shopping. Revenues are generated through a mixture of e-commerce, sponsorship and advertising. Break-even is anticipated to be towards the end of 2003.

Handbag.com has quickly established itself as the most popular women's website among UK female Internet users. Emphasizing the advantage in e-commerce of being a first mover. In its first three months it had received over 300,000 individual users.

As handbag and vavo.com suggest, building an e-brand demands that you really understand who your brand is aimed at. You must develop relationships and the more personal the better. The trouble is that personal attention is not that easy to produce. If it becomes too mechanical it is counterproductive, and as a customer you get the feeling of being part of an automatic system.

An interesting solution to this is to let your customers help each other to produce personal attention. Communities built through chat thrive on the Web. The Internet started life with newsgroups and interest groups chatting. The culture remains. The Web is a forum, an ongoing discussion, in which you can publish yourself.

In the most up-to-date technology, such as that invented by Dobedo (www.dobedo.co.uk), chat has developed into a kind of on-line party where you create your own personality (not necessarily your real one) and interact with others. Apart from just making conversation you can perform symbolized activities, like smiling, kissing, inviting someone for a drink, or going with someone to a private room for a more intimate interaction.

All these are examples of how 'live' the interactions will be on the Web in the future, with live video and, when the speed on the Net permits, perhaps the possibility of transferring physical experiences.

If you are already thinking along these lines, you will be more able to create a dynamic forum for customer interaction. What is most important is that you are able to offer and facilitate an experience that results in stimulating on-going communication between people.

Involvement is everything

LETSBUYIT.COM IS A NEW take on the shopping co-operative. The Swedish company has rolled out its online version of collective bargaining – co-buying – across Europe. In order to participate customers must first become members by registering at the website. LetsBuyIt is able to offer keen prices on its goods, ranging from kitchen appliances to holidays by sourcing direct from the supplier. The company has 50,000 suppliers, and the figure is rising steadily. This is a common business model widely adopted across the Internet. LetsBuyIt goes one step further, harnessing group purchasing power to get the best price possible.

Members join other members in expressing an interest to buy a particular product. The more people who sign up to buy, the cheaper the goods become. Typically the price will move down through three price bands as demand increases. If a member wishes to buy something they can check an onscreen graphic to see how many people have joined the co-buy so far and how many more are required to push the price down into the next band. Members enter their co-bid as either the current price or the best price. Obviously these are the same when the product's price has reached its lowest. If a member selects best price and this is not reached by the end of the co-buy period – each co-buy runs for a set time – then there is no purchase.

The participation of members goes beyond joining co-buys. Members can suggest goods to be put up on the LetsBuyIt website or goods they have found elsewhere on the net. The company also extends its service to online communities, where there is likely to be common demand for particular types of product.

LetsBuyIt is proof that involvement is all – whether it is involving the people in your organization or your customers. Never hesitate to ask the customer to produce something, with you or for you. 'Tell me and I'll forget, show me and I'll understand, involve me and I remember,' runs a Chinese proverb.

Involving customers in *product development* is especially useful as it can give you ideas for changes to existing products or new ones. I suggested that Scandinavian Airlines ask its passengers for advice about service – more as a marketing activity than actually for product development reasons – only to be astonished to find out how the busiest business-people tirelessly answered 80 questions, with total answer rates of 40–50 per cent, in exchange for a music CD or something similar. People are much more willing to participate than you normally expect – use that fact to create relationships.

You can also ask your customers and prospects to inform you about what your *competitors* are doing. Ask them openly for information; make them a part of your organization.

A third way is to ask your customers to find new customers for you by giving you the names of their friends. This has been used by mail order and financial services companies for years, but it has always has felt a little awkward in other businesses. This is no longer the case. With the Web this contact can be much more personal. It is easy for someone to give you the e-mail address of a friend for you to contact. (The compensation for this need not be extravagant. Instead it should create more involvement – such as a year's free subscription to your site if relevant, or someone else's site, or a magazine.)

Let me entertain you

INVOLVEMENT AND RELATIONSHIPS can be sparked off by providing customers with entertainment. Bringing a smile to people's faces creates a bond.

Little wonder then that in the entertainment business branding is a critical ingredient for success. In this industry there is usually a window of marketing with a definite beginning and an equally definite ending, a sort of time-framed branding project. In most other businesses the assumption is that the brand has to live for ever. A brand never lives for ever though it might live for a very long time, or be reactivated after a down period. But perceiving your brand as a having a five- to ten-year life, as in the entertainment business, gives you another, shorter, and more realistic ambition to work with. You may then be able to maximize your business within that perspective, rather than trying to stretch it out for ever.

In high-tech and Internet businesses, the compact market window is already a reality. For companies like 3Com with its very successful PalmPilot, the lifecycle of its products (PalmPilot, PalmII, PalmIII, PalmIV, PalmV) has strong similarities with the film industry. Every year there has to be another sequel.

One of the great entertainment brands of recent years was *Jurassic Park*. The brand empire of this seven–year-old brand is worth $450 million a year even though the film itself grossed only $1.5 billion. There are home videos, theme-park rides, collector's cups with McDonald's dino-sized meals, toys from Hasbro, followed by film sequels like *The Lost World*. The total value of all Jurassic Park brand sales up to 1999 was $5 billion. Without very well-defined brand values this would not have been possible.

While it is a tremendous advantage to be able to launch your brand values with a movie, the film world uses many ideas from other industries and has become very professional and structured in its marketing. Other industries could also learn a lot from the way films are branded.

There are many more examples of very successful films that have created new markets and branded businesses. *Notting Hill*, a film starring Julia Roberts and Hugh Grant, made a whole area of London extremely trendy and increased real-estate values. Now every second visitor to Notting Hill tries to find out exactly where the bookshop was; and of course, the coffee shop on the corner, portrayed in the film, is a real goldmine.

Similarly, *Titanic* reactivated the moribund cruise industry – somewhat bizarrely as the film was about one of the most tragic catastrophes in the history of passenger shipping. Cruises are now more popular than ever before, and new luxury cruise liners are being built. To the industry's extreme joy, it is the young who want to experience a little bit of cruise ship luxury. *Titanic II* is not a film sequel but a cruise liner that will be a near-exact copy of the sunken ship. It will be launched in 2002 and most of its cruises for the first few years are reported to be sold out.

Branding Hollywood-style also features product placement, simply placing your product in the hands of a film hero – a BMW for James Bond, or Nokia phones for the heroes of trendy action film *The Matrix*. This brings some complications. There is usually a conflict of interest between the brand owner, the director, and the actors when it comes to delivering value for the huge amount of money normally spent.

Product placement is increasingly old hat. Now companies want to have a deeper involvement. They may even want to tinker with the script to communicate the spiritual dimension of their brand or their long-term brand mission. This approach is only really suitable for the brand leader in a particular category – though, since the effect doesn't necessarily limit itself to one brand, it might change or develop the perception of consumers in an entire industry.

An emergent issue the entertainment industry will have to deal with is zapping, as viewers flit from channel to channel. For commercial media channels and advertisers this is a nightmare. If they are to work, advertisements must grab people's attention as never before. The same applies to advertising on the Internet. You will have to find new and innovative ways to touch your audiences. You will have to entertain them.

The logic is simple. Who do you want to be with? Someone who entertains you. Entertainment is integral to the attitude of the Net, and this will affect other audiences too; the older Web users will become strongly influenced by the younger generations in this respect. That is why traditional

Hollywood and branding

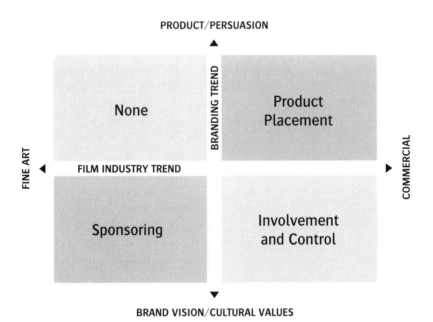

ways of selling will not be successful on the Net. We will see a totally new type of marketing, which will feel conspicuously free, easy, entertaining, and fun. The traditional marketing person will ask: what is the message? when does the selling (or teaching, or whatever) start? In this confusion, the metaphor, the story, the game, the show, the play, and the movie will be new sales tools; traditional product arguments and comparisons will have to stand back.

Entertainment is not pure frivolity. It is another way to produce value. If you are giving the customer another reason for buying from you, in addition to getting the expected product or service delivered, you are adding value. If I have a choice of buying something from a bore who is neglecting me as a customer, or from someone who makes the whole thing fun, interesting, or memorable, why should I choose the bore? I might even be prepared to pay a little more in return.

Sometimes being entertaining can be a bit too demanding, if you are supposed to play games or spend a lot of time chatting, etc. The best marketing entertainment will be integrated with your purpose in visiting the site in question. For instance, when the Swedish house-paint company

Alcro (www.alcro.se) helps me choose the right colours and the right kind of paint for my house in a very entertaining way, it's a lot of fun and very useful. Similarly, when you are able to assemble the car, computer, or vacation you want, it's fun and productive at the same time.

Copying the entrepreneur

THE ESSENCE OF e-branding and the new realities is that branding has embraced an entrepreneurial element. Previously branding theory and entrepreneurialism were poles apart. Now, they embrace each other like long-lost friends.

Entrepreneurs with a real flair for brand building and communication don't usually need a handbook or a method. Like a good conductor, they know exactly how to orchestrate people and organizations to produce a performance that will be perceived by customers to be in harmony with their expectations of value, usually outperforming less well-orchestrated competitors.

These people are exceptional. In most cases, the brand consultant, or tools and methods, or a book like this, can be invaluable. For instance, you may be a great leader but not possess a special talent for branding (maybe you have entrepreneurial talent in other areas). You could be part of a group of entrepreneurs who are supposed to work as a team. Or you could be an employed manager who has to feel as if you own your business in order to be really successful.

In all these situations, the ideas, methods, and toolkit presented in this book will help you either to get off to a flying start, or to continue on the path you have already taken. You will be able to have the same ownership over your core values, the focus, and personalization in your corporate brand, as the most successful of the entrepreneurial superbrands.

Branding literature remains largely theoretical because of the mystery inherent in the subject. A successful brand like Nike, for instance, is almost magical in comparison with its competitors. For academics, the inevitable temptation is to dissect and analyze the science of the power that superbrands hold in people's minds.

Of course, it is interesting to know why things work. But it is more important to know that it does work and how you can make it happen in your own business. Maybe the most important reason for approaching the issue of branding in a structured way is the fact that the key to successful branding in most cases is kept in the mind of one person – the entrepreneur.

In many larger organizations there is surprisingly little documentation of what the company stands for – you would look in vain for core values or a Brand Code. But you can and must understand and document the very soul of your brand.

The innocence of Virgin

IF YOU WANT the personification of the brand builder as entrepreneur look no further than Richard Branson, founder and chairman of Virgin. No one person has ever created more awareness around a brand. According to a recent survey, 96 per cent of British consumers have heard of Virgin and 95 per cent can correctly name Richard Branson as its founder. Today he can look at a brand that has moved into and transformed almost 25 types of businesses. The brand's recognition and strength have largely come about because of him.

Branson has actually followed much the same approach since the very start of his business career. In an interview in *Vogue* in 1968, Branson said 'I want to create a company which will do all sorts of different things for different people, it doesn't matter what we're doing, it is the way we are going to do it that is going to matter. It is going to be all about doing things in a way that challenges the markets, you know less dodgy than things are done at the moment in this country.' He also talked about the fact 'that one day we are going to have this brand that crosses all these different areas and does all these different things.'

First there was the record company – responsible the biggest selling record of the 1970s, *Tubular Bells*; and later home to the Sex Pistols, the Rolling Stones, the Human League, and Culture Club. Then Branson toyed with all sorts of companies through the late 1970s and 1980s – Virgin this and Virgin that – but none of them got very far. The company really didn't have the resources or the money or the management capability. But by the mid-1980s the record company was highly profitable, and that's really when the serious brand diversification began. Branson decided to go into the airline business. His aim was to create an airline that would be different, that would challenge the marketplace. A profusion of brand extensions have followed – Virgin is a rail company, an ISP, a cola maker, a financial services company, a mobile phone company, and much more.

Virgin succeeds because it stands for something. Branson says that any new product or service must be, or have the prospect of becoming in the future:

The best quality
Innovative
Good value for money
Challenging to existing alternatives
Something that adds a sense of fun or cheekiness

Virgin claims that nine out of ten projects it considers are potentially very profitable, but, if they don't fit with the group's values, they are rejected.[4] Nevertheless, says Branson, 'If an idea satisfies at least four of these five criteria, we'll usually take a serious look at it.'

What are we to make of this? If you know what you stand for, it is much easier to make efficient decisions. The framework of reference to make the decisions is already in place, providing a brand compass that helps managers make rapid evaluations.

Instead of being stamped with the idea of a product, the Virgin brand has become stamped with personality and values. According to Will Whitehorn, director of corporate communications and one of Branson's closest lieutenants, 'It is remarkably so that because of the airline and because of Virgin Records, because of the Megastores, because of all sorts of things that we've done and markets we've entered, in the UK it has become the public's perception of the brand. People don't associate Virgin with just anything. They associate Virgin with a set of ideas – fun, value, and innovation – and it has got incredible strength here. Actually in the market where we've developed the brand very consciously, such as in Japan, it is also an incredibly strong brand. It is one of the few foreign brands that has captured the imagination in that country. In countries where we're only trading in a couple of things, like the US, Virgin is seen more as a sort of airline brand. Although a lot of people have heard of Virgin Records, it's known that we've got Megastores, big ones in places like Times Square, so the association is slowly changing.'

When Virgin takes over an existing business or enters a new market, its values are there as prerequisites, but it can take years to achieve the benefit of the values in the businesses it creates. The values are guiding principles within the businesses, standing as the foundation for the brand and its communication. When going into a new market or creating a new product, the entire business plan is constructed around the ability to fulfil as many of those aspects of the brand as possible. Will Whitehorn expresses this

Virgin Brand Mind Space

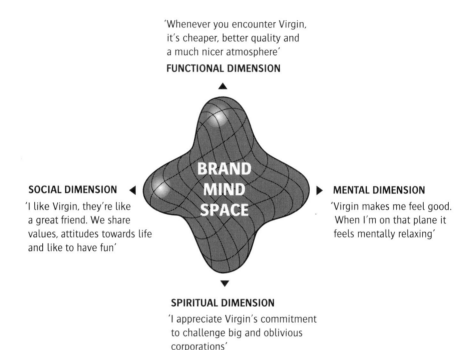

'Whenever you encounter Virgin,
it's cheaper, better quality and
a much nicer atmosphere'
FUNCTIONAL DIMENSION

BRAND MIND SPACE

SOCIAL DIMENSION
'I like Virgin, they're like
a great friend. We share
values, attitudes towards life
and like to have fun'

MENTAL DIMENSION
'Virgin makes me feel good.
When I'm on that plane it
feels mentally relaxing'

SPIRITUAL DIMENSION
'I appreciate Virgin's commitment
to challenge big and oblivious
corporations'

as 'a way of using the brand as a management tool, and very few companies work that way.'

THE FUNCTIONAL DIMENSION

On the functional dimension the Virgin brand is undoubtedly perceived as delivering good quality, cheap prices, and a well-liked and challenging style of doing business. This of course is part of the brand's strength; as an intangible brand, the stronger the perceived benefit of the functional attributes the more sustainable it will be.

THE MENTAL DIMENSION

An individual passenger flying Virgin Atlantic has the perception that it makes them 'feel good,' that the experience of choosing and using Virgin contributes in someway to their peace of mind. Although in reality sitting on the plane and travelling from one destination to another is a physical experience, the main point is that it's satisfying to know you've chosen this brand for how it makes you feel – the brand does something other than merely take you to your destination.

THE SOCIAL DIMENSION

A brand like Virgin is strong on the social dimension, reflecting its ability to create a loyal following among customers and the media. Virgin challenges the marketplace with a youthful and almost mischievous approach that reflects the way customers want to act themselves, hence by choosing Virgin customers display their own values and attitude to life. If the Virgin philosophy appeals to customers in one market segment, say airlines, they're also likely to choose Virgin in another market.

THE SPIRITUAL DIMENSION

Virgin's proposition to 'challenge the market' is well rooted in the spiritual dimension. Its conscious way of creating better and improved market conditions for customers shows its commitment to providing change and purposely shaking up the system to benefit everybody in society. Virgin challenges big and unshakeable corporations, making its own business solutions flexible and fun for customers.

Branding for the future

IN THIS CONSTANTLY changing world ruled by wired-up entrepreneurs, the future can seem a million years away. When the present is impossible to understand, who wants to embrace the future? Most of our best-performing brands are made for today – they are not really prepared for tomorrow. But we must embrace the future now before it is upon us. Today's new realities are tomorrow's conditions for entry.

The brands of tomorrow are the ones we haven't heard of yet. A friend told me about going into a trendy jeans shop and asking for the jeans that the kids, the teenagers, were buying. The young woman in the shop looked at him, amused, and pointed to the back of the store where he found at least seven or eight brands of jeans he had never heard of. He couldn't find Levis, or Wranglers, or Lee. The brands of the future are out back and you have never heard of them.

Levis is an interesting case of a brand searching for its future. After a glorious run in the 1980s, positioning 501s as the authentic jeans with sex appeal, the company became both a victim of its own success and, ironically, a fashion victim. Young people stopped wearing jeans as an expression of youthful freedom because their parents, encouraged by Levis, were still wearing them. A recent article about Levis observed 'If they can make it another two or three years in the market, they will probably be retro.'

Old brands regularly find new audiences, though it is seldom planned and the audience is usually not the one anticipated. Levis might have chosen to stay with its baby-boomer die-hard customers, or to try to reinvent itself for the younger generation. At present, it seems to have fallen between two stools. Its brand values are intimately linked to the once rebellious people born in the 1960s, which, of course, alienates the younger rebels.

Another brand tied to the same audience is Harley-Davidson, which had a very tough time in the 1980s but is now tremendously successful, a cult brand with consumers who can afford to pay what it costs to own a Harley. The average age of its customers today is 42, compared to 32 ten years ago. The brand is benefiting from a new breed of professionals – accountants, lawyers and stockbrokers, who don motorcycle leathers at the weekend in search of freedom and another life away from the office. (Customers buying their first motorcycle or coming back to riding after a lapse increased more than threefold between 1987 and 1994.) In 1997, the company enjoyed record sales of $1.75 billion, on 132,000 motorcycles, and commanded a hefty 48 per cent share of the North American market for heavy road bikes (which is showing healthy growth of between 8 and 10 per cent a year). Orders outstrip production, creating a waiting list for many models. Year-old Harleys sell for 25 per cent more than the list price of brand new ones.[5]

Maybe Levis should have continued to exploit and develop its brand among its old fans, rather than aiming for a younger audience that choose new brands with values that are important for them – like the ironic consumerism of Diesel, one of many new jeans brands of today (or already yesterday).

Future-driven brands remain a rarity. Few companies think this way. Strangely, many brand-building tools and programs ignore the future. This might be because of uncertainty about what the future holds. This is a cop-out. Brands and everyone involved in them must buy into the future with total commitment and with the total commitment of their imaginations.

The future will demand more of brands. The future is being shaped by transparency in the marketplace – with better-informed, more critical consumers, internationalization, e-commerce, and so on. The brand that wants to assure its future will have to stand for something, not just be pleasing to everybody. It will be open to joint ventures, brand partnerships, or co-branding; and ingredient branding, leveraging the strengths of different brands to create a single solution or offer, will also be an important strategy. Tomorrow's brands will have to challenge the customer's creativity, entertain, and at the same time deliver quality and reliability.

In this new world, the brand will be the main carrier of values and associations. If these are clearly defined and expressed, the brand will be a more efficient way than consumer segmentation to find your target audience. In fact, the audience will find the brand, not the other way around. That is the key to the Internet. It is akin to a play's audience taking the stage and inventing their own drama. The brand will segment its own market, without using demographic or geographic data or consumer patterns as a base.

The brand will make friends with some customers, who will then act as ambassadors and advocates. But it will also repel other customers, who don't like the brand's attitude. Thus the strength of the friendship between the brand and its customers – its users – will determine the brand's strength, both in marketing terms and in financial valuation. The future belongs to the brand.

"I don't know the key to success, but the key to failure is to try to please everyone"

Bill Cosby

AUTHENTIC REPRODUCTION

Friendship branding

SO FAR, WE HAVE looked at the basics of branding and the new realities affecting the world of branding. It is clear that the basic principles as well as the realities are in a perpetual state of development. Sparks may fly as branding is reshaped, like hot metal, in front of our eyes.

Today's branding is different from yesterday's and definitely different from tomorrow's. In order to understand fully how brands work *on* us, and how to make them work efficiently *for* us with others, it helps to think about branding as friendship. I know this sounds corny, but suspend your skepticism, because the relationship between a brand and loyal customer has many similarities with the relationship between a pair of friends. It is also a good model for the future.

Let us experiment. Close your eyes and think of a friend. Imagine your friend in detail in front of you – the more detail the better. Take your time.

Now ask yourself, do you always think the same as your friend? Do you always agree about everything? Or do you often have a totally different view on things? Do you sometimes laugh at your friend? Maybe it's not an evil laugh, maybe it's friendly, but you laugh all the same.

If I ask 50 people this in a seminar, most of them agree. You don't always think the same as your friends, you sometimes even laugh at them. But we still respect them for being our friends. What is the concept of friendship based on?

The definition of friendship could be that, at a deep level, we SHARE VALUE.

Here's another experiment. Try to put into words the values that you share with the friend you just saw in front of you. You'll find this very difficult, amazingly difficult. It will probably take you quite a while to come up with a list of values. And, once you have it on paper, you will be disappointed. The words will be the same as you imagine anybody else could say about any friend. Somehow you would have liked your list, for your particular friend, to be different and personal – unique even, as your friendship is.

What you just have experienced in your mind is a very clear demonstration of how difficult it is to work with brands. If you describe the value of a brand to others you will try to do it verbally, and you will find that the words you use are very generic – they could be used for any brand (and for describing any of your friends, too, for that matter). At the same time, you know that one of the most important ways to succeed in the market is to be different.

There are two ways to avoid this problem. One is to use other forms of communication: pictures or sounds. (When I am working on establishing a Brand Code, I always hold a visual workshop.) But still it can be difficult to transfer your particular associations and connotations about a brand value. So what you end up doing is talking to each other a lot about 'what we really mean.' You painfully work through every nuance of every value attached to the brand until your collective voice boxes ache with the effort. The humble act of holding multiple conversations is the most important part of the process of building a consistent brand in an organization. Talk, then talk some more.

Let's think more about the friendship model for building brands. Crucial to this is SHOWING INTEREST in your customers. You could compare this to so-called friends who show very little interest in you, but expect everyone to pay attention when they discuss the minutiae of their own life.

A very important difference between successful and less successful brands is the interest that successful brands show in their customers. It is usually small, easy, and not very costly things that symbolize a lot for customers.

When Volvo sponsored a golf tournament, it let everyone driving a Volvo park close to the tee. All other car brands were consigned to distant parking lots. When Nokia sponsored a rock concert, those who showed their Nokia mobile phone at the door received free admission. Even more efficient is a phone call from a telephone operator to confirm that the installation you have just had done was successful and to your satisfaction. Or when a car salesperson calls you after three years and makes an offer for your car.

There is nothing smart or complicated about these examples. Indeed, the reverse is true. All these ideas sound quite natural, but are seldom experienced by customers. Showing interest doesn't have to be a sleazy direct marketing letter misspelling your address or using the wrong name. At its best the customer finds it appropriate, even reassuring. It supports what they already felt about the brand. It confirms that their confidence in the brand was well placed.

This becomes even more important when customers are distant. For Net brands it is crucial. For example, Jeff Bezos, founder of Amazon.com, had the brilliant idea of suggesting other books that readers of the book you just bought have also ordered. Although this facility is automatic and routine, it still feels like someone is thinking about you. And furthermore, Amazon.com keeps on offering you books that fit your profile. To get that experience in a real bookshop you would have to be a very well-known, regular customer.

Being taken by surprise by a friend builds a stronger bond between you. A telephone call from someone you know offering you tickets to a football game or the theatre, asking if you would like to join them for a drink beforehand – that's one of the best ways to strengthen a friendship. And the same goes for building a lasting brand relationship.

Amazon.com, again, surprised me after I had placed my first order by sending me a coffee mug for Christmas, to keep my coffee warm while reading. I'm now one of their most enthusiastic customers, although they have many competitors clamouring for my attention.

The star of Starbucks

THE ORIGINAL STARBUCKS was founded in 1971 in Seattle by Jerry Baldwin and Gordon Bowker, a literature major and a writer passionately committed to world-class coffee and dedicated to educating customers about the legacy of the drink. It was in the 1960s, at Peets Coffee, that Baldwin had discovered the romance of coffee. In the mid-1950s Alfred Peet had introduced America to the arabica coffee bean, dark roasted to ensure a full-bodied flavour. Americans, thus far, had been used to an inferior type of coffee made from the robusta coffee bean, mostly produced and sold in cans. The Europeans treated the robusta bean as a cheap commodity.

Howard Schultz, now CEO of Starbucks, joined the small company in Seattle in 1982. He brought with him a vision and values, and he had a mission. He saw Starbucks not for what it was, but for what it could be. With a competitive drive and desire to make sure everyone in the organization could win together, he set out to blend coffee with romance, to dare to achieve what others said was impossible. He asked himself how it would feel to build a business and really own the equity of a brand, not just collect a pay check. He saw the potential in bringing great coffee to all Americans, to spread Starbucks' excitement about coffee beans beyond Seattle. The Starbucks name could become synonymous with great coffee – and eventually a brand that would guarantee world-class quality.

Up until 1984 Starbucks' core business was to sell high-quality coffee beans. Coffee was treated as a commodity product to be sold to customers who would bring the beans home as groceries. Shultz knew that the real potential lay in becoming more than merely a commodity. Starbucks could encompass something else, a great experience rather than just another retail store. In 1985 Shultz set up a new type of store, Il Giornale, to serve coffee by the cup and espresso drinks.

In 1987 Schultz had the opportunity to buy Starbucks' assets for $4 million, including the name and the roasting plant. This would complement the Il Giornale coffee beverage business. And, as promised to investors, the new company had to expand rapidly, opening 125 new stores in five years, with the goal to go public, a task completed in 1989.

According to Howard Schultz, it is impossible to reinvent a company's culture. Values, which constitute the base of a culture, are instilled from the very beginning, and the company's guiding principles have to be implanted early so that they function as guidance for every decision, hire, and every strategic objective. There needs to be authenticity in every aspect of the business. Starbucks has been created as a company with a competitive advantage based on its values and guiding principles.

Today, Starbucks conducts itself and its business according to the following values:

unshakeable integrity,
disarming honesty,
and authenticity in every aspect
of the business.

To help the organization apply these values actively, they are embodied in its mission statement, which is an interpretation or translation of the values into a set of guiding principles held in common.

THE STARBUCKS MISSION STATEMENT

Establish Starbucks as the premier purveyor of the finest coffee in the world while maintaining our uncompromising principles as we grow. The following six guiding principles will help us measure the appropriateness of our decisions:

- Provide a great work environment and treat each other with respect and dignity. Embrace diversity as an essential component of the way we do business.

- Apply the highest standards of excellence to the purchasing, roasting, and fresh delivery of our coffee.

- Develop enthusiastically satisfied customers all of the time.

- Contribute positively to our communities and our environment.

- Recognize that profitability is essential to our future success.

This is a powerful message of purpose and an organic body of beliefs, and as such it is a guiding tool for the organization. For Starbucks it is also viewed as a powerful energizer that can grow the enterprise into something far greater than one leader could envision. For the Starbucks brand it supports setting the criteria for how the brand should be communicated, with manifest upsides like a strengthened bond with customers.

If the values interpreted in the mission statement are the fundamental groundwork for the way the organization moves, how should we interpret the brand? Starbucks is not just a cup of coffee that you can smell or taste. It's about a relationship with a friend. It was only after years of great customer relationships that Starbucks became a brand. As Mike Sweeney puts it: 'It's just that suddenly somebody recognizes that these relationships exists and calls it a brand. The human condition in America and Italy is the same. So, I think while Starbucks has educated America about coffee, it hasn't been in the way of a schoolteacher, it's just been part of a shared journey and making ourselves available and as customers make themselves available, it's the relationship again.'

A relationship with a friend is built on trust, which is fundamental for Starbucks. It has gained the trust of its customers through its commitment to making coffee that is the best of its kind and providing it with dedication. This is what builds the relationship between Starbucks and its customers. It is very hard to develop a good relationship with someone with whom you don't have a sense of shared values. There seems to be a level of caring at Starbucks that most companies don't reach, and it understands the fundamentals of building a friendship with its customers.

What constitutes the Starbucks brand and what does it say? As Mike Sweeney describes it, 'Exhale, I think that's the essence of it. As the world gets busier, there is an opposite reaction; every force has an equal and opposite reaction. And the opposite reaction is an increased need for sanctuary and quiet, and Starbucks has been chosen by customers, around the world, certainly in North America, as a place where they can find sanctuary and it becomes a very important place in people's lives. It's thoughtful and caring and nurturing, and that's what many people find here. It's a soft chair, a hot cup of coffee next to a warm fire on a cold night, and that's valuable. That is one of the things that keep us all focused on what we do. It seems to be a universal need though, a universal truth, it goes back to the idea of the human condition of finding some place of quiet.'

The Starbucks brand as defined by Sweeney is really about the coffee break. And sometimes that coffee break comes in a takeaway cup. But what's in that cup is a little bit of peace of mind. Sometimes, perhaps, it's a simple indulgence, knowing that you've got the best coffee in the world.

A brand in Starbucks' way of thinking is really just a web of relationships between the company, the partners, and the customers. This relationship is based on a set of values and beliefs about the world. The brand exists because Starbucks' customers created it. As Sweeney observes: 'Companies rarely create the brands, they initiate them and the customers then create the brands, because a brand is a relationship.'

Starbucks is the antithesis of the big American company, which is often seen as the evil empire arriving to take over. It claims simply to make its product available and the product isn't just the coffee, it's the environment and the relationship that creates the brand. So far when going outside America, the company has found that the same holds true; people want a sanctuary, they want a quiet place to get together with friends, or to be alone.

Of course there are differences in traditions and customs, but you also find that people are the same around the world; they want and aspire to the same things. The original idea with Starbucks had been to provide a quick stand-up to-go service in downtown locations. The focus then turned to customer service, moving away from the sometimes criticized product orientation to the service aspect, 'to fill souls' in a setting that was positioned as a third place or extended living room, and hence the customer experience became vital.

One issue on which Howard Schultz has not been keen to budge is franchising. He has always argued that if it did this Starbucks could not guarantee quality, which is at the core of the business, even though franchising would be the logical route to national expansion. Competitors who did franchise never developed a strong brand, and in Starbucks' eyes a franchiser stands between them and the customer. Consequently, company-owned stores was a way for Starbucks to guarantee that its vision and value system is understood. However, it is apparent that Starbucks has now compromised on this, since it has licensing agreements with airports and hotels, although this represents less than 10 per cent of outlets.

To keep true to its ideals while expanding the brand, Starbucks requires discipline and a delicate sense of balance. Sweeney notes, 'I think it's successful, however there are no discussions within Starbucks that go on longer and with more passion than whether or not we should enter or renew a partnership with another company. It is about being personal, and how that's creating relationships. It's not just stamping it out, it doesn't work if you don't have passion or if you don't really believe in the things I've been talking about, that's the magic – it's the belief. If it's simply a deal to someone, we are less interested, they would really have to understand what Starbucks is about, share that value that we attribute to what we're doing here, and act like we would act. We take that more seriously than anything else we do.'

The equity of the Starbucks brand is a priceless asset, and every decision made in the company has to contribute to its sustainability and differentiation. If Starbucks can capture the imagination with new, innovative products, the brand can become larger than life, according to Howard Schultz. But at all times Starbucks has to make sure that nothing it does dilutes the integrity of the brand. Branded partnerships or brand extensions can be successful only when people have come to trust the brand.

The intention with Starbucks was never to build a brand; the goal was to build a great company, one that stood for something, one that valued the authenticity of its product and the passion of its people. Howard Schultz gets a lot of praise for bringing the Starbucks brand into the (American) national consciousness so quickly. The secret of the power of the Starbucks brand is the passion and the commitment of the partners, who are the true ambassadors of the coffee and for the brand; they in turn connect Starbucks to the customers. It is interesting to observe a company that uses its brand so vividly as a management tool and consistently works with it as a focal point.

It is authenticity and continual care that will make a brand like Starbucks last. Brand loyalty was earned by educating one customer at a time. And if people believe they share values with a company, they will stay loyal to that brand. The evolution of Starbucks shows how a company can lead with its heart and still provide long-term value for shareholders, without sacrificing its core belief of treating its employees with respect and dignity.

Starbucks Brand Mind Space

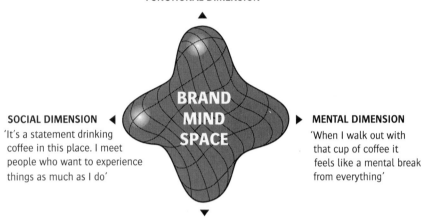

'Coffee at its finest, it's the atmosphere and the sence of dedication among the staff that's so special in this place'

FUNCTIONAL DIMENSION

SOCIAL DIMENSION
'It's a statement drinking coffee in this place. I meet people who want to experience things as much as I do'

BRAND MIND SPACE

MENTAL DIMENSION
'When I walk out with that cup of coffee it feels like a mental break from everything'

SPIRITUAL DIMENSION
'The fact that Starbucks care about bringing coffee from all different places around the world to us is great. We get to learn about the origins of that country's culture'

THE FUNCTIONAL DIMENSION

The functional dimension displays what the perception of an experience brand could look like. It is the highest quality coffee, cared for by dedicated partners who brew it with knowledge and in a dedicated manner, creating a friendly and special atmosphere for the customers.

THE MENTAL DIMENSION

In the mental dimension the perception about Starbucks is as a place to experience a mental break from the hassles of daily life. With that cup of coffee you either bring that feeling with you outside, or inhale the experience at the local Starbucks.

THE SOCIAL DIMENSION

You take a stand by just walking inside a Starbucks, a social hangout or club for people who appreciate the experience of discovery, aspiration, and great service. A brand like this a bearer of lifestyle attributes, a social insignia on the streets and in the workplace. Think about the green banner around each cup of Starbucks served, almost as recognized as the Nike swoosh, at least in America.

THE SPIRITUAL DIMENSION

The cultural aspect of coffee is at the heart of the Starbucks experience. Entering a Starbucks coffee shop, customers become aware of the cultural origins of coffee, specific countries' customs, and so on. The partners at Starbucks can take on the role of guides in the jungle of tastes, while providing different coffees in an exciting atmosphere.

Tightening relationships

SUCCESSFUL BRANDS KNOW how to tighten the relationship with their customers. They do things *with* their customers. Does this ring a bell? This is exactly what happens when human friendships begin. Shared memories of the things we did together are incredibly potent.

So when American car manufacturers have homecoming parties for their cars (or owners) at their factory, it's an irresistible activity for many owners. Buying a new car is an enduring memory, one that binds the owner to the brand. A staggering 45,000 turned up at the Saturn factory to celebrate.

Launched in 1990, the Saturn was GM's first new nameplate since Chevrolet and has turned into a branding triumph. The car itself is fairly spartan. The Saturn has good price points and appeals to the consumers' emotions by being identified with the heritage of hard-working values. Most persuasively, the Saturn is backed by a terrific dealer network that provides truly differentiated sales with no haggling and high quality service.

Saturn has laid out what it calls its 'pricing principles.' 'No hassle means Saturn Retailers are up-front about all elements of a vehicle's price. No last minute add-ons or hidden charges. Nothing up our sleeves. No haggle means the retailer should stick to whatever price it sets. Horse trading and dickering don't fit with Saturn's Philosophy. No customer should ever wonder whether the Retailer's next customer will get a better price by "driving a harder bargain".'

None of this is accidental. Saturn's brand development focused on the buying experience, service and support, rather than being narrowly focused on the product. It was concerned with people and processes rather than the product.

According to research by J D Power, the three car brands in the US with the highest customer satisfaction are Lexus, Infiniti and Saturn. The link between them is that all have *de novo* dealer networks designed, developed and managed with an intense pursuit of consistent, exceptional customer service. In 1996, the Saturn was rated best in overall sales satisfaction among all car brands. It was rated seventh in customer satisfaction – the top six were all luxury cars – Lexus, Infiniti, Acura, Mercedes-Benz, Cadillac, and Jaguar. Customers even gave Saturn high marks on the service they received when their cars were recalled.

Contrast this with the problems GM has experienced elsewhere with dealerships featuring a variety of its models. In 1995, GM vice president Ronald L Zarrella wrote to 8,500 dealers pointing out, rather belatedly, that its autos were not commodities and offering them for sale next to competing brands was not what GM wanted. It was significant that while there are 8,500 US GM dealerships, there are 17,000 franchises. Individual dealers can have as many as six franchises operating from the same place. Saturn dealers have no such complications. Their onus on straight talking and value added service remains distinctive. They have created lasting friendships.

Relationships start young. Parents know the bond that never disappears between themselves and their children. If you are there at the birth, you are forever tied into the infant's experience and life. How about if you are at the birth of a car? It's not the same as your child, I admit, but some of the same principles apply. That's why Volkswagen plans to let new owners literally be there at the very birth of their car in the Dresden factory making its new super limousine. It is called the Glass Factory and the idea is that you go there and spend three to five hours actually seeing your own vehicle being assembled by workers. More than ordinary anonymous assembly-line workers, they will become actors on a stage – or midwives. Finally, you can drive your new car off the line.

The art of giving

FRIENDS DO THINGS together, and they do things for other people. If you are locked in a friendship, you may well find yourself helping and supporting a variety of causes. Encourage your customers to participate in making some contribution to society is an efficient way of gaining brand friends for life. This could be planting trees together as a paper company did with its customers, or something as simple as donating a couple of cents to the coffee farmers in Guatemala for every cup of coffee, as was the case at Starbucks.

Companies are now developing relationship programs that are directly related to their customers' conscience. There is a plethora of products pledging, if you buy them, to donate money to help save the rainforests or support medical research. Cause-related marketing is a potent new weapon in the battle for customers.

American Express first applied the technique in 1983 in support of a project to restore the Statue of Liberty – patriotism is a great loyalty builder. Since then, companies have linked promotions to a wide variety of causes, leveraging the buying decision with customers' existing and often strongly held loyalties. Cause-related marketing offers a win–win–win situation. The cause – be it a hospital, a charity, or the environment – gains directly; customers feel good about themselves, creating a more satisfying purchasing experience; and the company or brand benefits from the 'halo' effect, leading to greater loyalty. Such loyalty building creates a situation in which all sides come out well. At least, that's the theory.

Many airlines, among them British Airways, collect coins in different currencies on the plane as another small example of doing something with their customers. McDonald's collects customers' small change. The smallest things can be beautiful gestures. Their meaning is important. It is a good way to show that there are more important things in life; to show that the relationship between the brand and the customer can be something more than practical, user oriented, and businesslike. It makes your brand look more humane, and it makes your relationship with customers more important than one that is simply financial.

Loyal friends

ALL THIS AND MORE creates a really strong friendship between the brand and its customers. And the effect of such a friendship is LOYALTY. Customer loyalty is one of the most well-documented areas in business marketing literature. Almost everybody is aware of how important loyal customers are, certainly in theory. And we know how much it costs to acquire a new customer, and how long it takes to make that new customer as profitable as the old loyal customer who, without sales costs, keeps on purchasing your products or services. Recent research shows that if you increase your customer loyalty by 5 per cent you can gain 25 per cent in profit. The problem is that although everybody knows this, few companies actually seem to care – or, at least, to do anything about it.

On the contrary, many businesses treat their loyal customers very badly; they milk them for all they are worth, and humiliate them with extra costs. And all the while they are buying new customers' attention at a cost that destroys their profitability for many years to come – if they ever become customers, that is. This is habitual among media companies, magazines, cable TV operators, etc. New customers are treated with special rates, while loyal customers pay the full rate without any reductions. It suddenly seems too easy to count your losses if you 'give away' bonuses to loyal customers; whereas your prospects are not yet your customers, so by definition they can't be non-profitable. Talk about fooling yourself – this is corporate self-deception on a ridiculous scale.

However, some businesses have a long tradition of showing how much they value loyalty. Insurance companies are good examples of how to treat your existing long-term customers well by giving them bonuses. In contrast, telecom companies have yet to prove that they can handle this. With very few exceptions new clients are still kings, and by buying a new subscription you still get your mobile phone almost for free. Sensible customers change supplier on a regular basis. Much the same happens with financial services, where existing customers often pay to subsidize cheap mortgages for new customers.

Companies know that loyalty is important, but are unsure how to create it. Loyalty is earned. And it is here that many books about customer loyalty are severely lacking. It's just not enough to give bonuses or some extras.

To be really loyal as a customer, you have to feel like a friend, and to feel like a friend you have to be treated as one and sense that you share some values with the brand. You have to feel that your friendship is valued. Brands have to deliver long-term friendships. This involves everyone, not just the commission-based salesforce, but also service people, distributors, dealers, retailers, and so on, all along a business's service chain. To orchestrate this you need more than just the lyrics – fine words from managers and scripted customer responses – you need music and a conductor as well.

Real and perceived reality

CENTRAL TO FRIENDSHIP is our perception of people. Appearances can be deceptive. The people we instantly disliked when we first met them can become our warmest friends. In branding there is a similar confusion between reality and perceived reality. Things are not always as they seem.

In the mid-1980s, American car manufacturer Chrysler and Japanese car manufacturer Mitsubishi formed a joint venture in California to build a sports car. The cars that rolled off the assembly line were practically identical twins. The only noticeable difference between them was the nameplate, Mitsubishi Eclipse or Plymouth Laser. So far, so good.

The cars were offered to customers at basically the same price and through basically the same dealership structure. Here, real reality and perceived reality got to work. In the first year the Mitsubishi Eclipse outsold the Plymouth Laser by 52 per cent. In 1994, the last year both cars were marketed, the Mitsubishi could slap on a 24 per cent higher sticker price than that of the Plymouth. And in the same year when the research firm conducted its survey of user satisfaction among buyers of new cars, the Plymouth had six times more complaints than the Mitsubishi.

Two cars, two brands – one reality, one perceived reality. What a difference a nameplate can make. The Plymouth Laser is no more; the Mitsubishi Eclipse is as popular as ever.

The question of real reality versus perceived reality gets you deep into the philosophical mire. Philosophers such as the German Immanuel Kant claimed that there is only a personally perceived reality. He reasoned that we all perceive a table, for instance, in very different ways; we have only learned to *describe* it in a similar way. If the table is made of wood and we knock on it, the sound that is produced sounds different in each individual person's ears and mind, the feeling of its surface is also perceived differently, and so on. Based on that, Kant claimed that there might be an objective reality – 'Das Ding an sich' – but it would never be perceived in exactly the same way by any two human beings. In everyday life this would definitely be impractical. Who, for instance, would want to be the owner of physical items in a world with no objective reality? Probably no one.

But the truth is that if you are going to be successful in branding, you have to adopt a little of that kind of attitude and thinking. And that is easier said than done. Our lives are earthbound to such a degree that we seem to fall back on the concept of real reality all the time. We need to break free from the gravity of real reality so that we are able to orbit in a cosmos of the perceived. Maybe the new technology offering us computerized virtual reality will help us as a metaphor and train our minds to accept perceived reality as a completely normal condition. Who knows?

I personally find it difficult to make the transition between real and perceived reality. Although I have worked in communication for over 20 years, and have held numerous seminars about the important difference between these two worlds, it is still hard for me. I tend to fall back on and talk about real reality when I know that the solution is completely in the domain of the perceived.

In the typical industrial business culture, real reality always wins over the perceived. For instance, when talking about quality the total focus is on the real reality aspect of it – how materials, components, or the actual process of production can be improved – usually ending up in very costly change programs. There is only limited interest in the perception side of quality – what customers actually perceive and why they do so.

I have seen cases when no real change in service has been perceived as an improvement just because the company has stated its ambition to be better on service. The communication about service was actually enough for many customers to perceive a change in service quality. Your expectation as a customer is, of course, very important. If you expect a very high service level, you tend to be very critical even if the provider of the service is investing heavily in real reality improvements. And it's not as easy as exchanging real reality improvements with perceived reality measures. Usually you will need to do both; or at least, make some visual improvements that support the perceived idea of a product that is now better.

When Nokia launched a small, silver steel-plated mobile phone, it was the first of its kind to look really different from other mobile phones. It looked much more like a cigarette case or a powder compact. The Nokia 8110, as this model was called, was an immediate success. Customers were willing to pay three times as much for this phone as for the identical package in a more ordinary, but still slim casing. Nokia had not only created a great commercial product, but had also invested in building the brand. Even customers not able to buy the small silver phone regarded it as a statement of values from Nokia. 'It's typical Nokia, and that's just the kind of brand I like,' they reasoned.

Despite being a technology-driven company, Nokia understood the power of perceived reality and put a great deal of effort into design and appearance. Engineering companies tend to put a high priority on real reality, since this is where the true challenge exists for an engineer.

Many high-tech companies have no choice in this. If you don't pursue rapid technical development in your field, you shouldn't be in business at all. But some of the most astonishing commercially successful high-tech products are not examples of a mind-blowing technology that impresses the customers. Rather, it's the packaging, the look and feel of the product, that makes it come alive. This was the case with the Nokia 8110. The much cheaper 6110 had the latest data communication features that the more expensive phone lacked. But 8110 customers didn't seem to mind at all.

This is also the case with 3Com's PalmPilot. The technology presented by 3Com was not at all new or revolutionary; Apple had introduced a couple of pen-based computers years before. Instead, it was the size and the style – how it was packaged to the consumer – and the feeling it created among its users. You actually looked smart using your pen rather than awkwardly fingering a mini keyboard.

In many other areas of business you can learn a lot from high-tech people. They live in a highly competitive world; their product life cycles are short; they have access to the same basic components and software technologies. It's very much an application game: packaging your product, making it appeal to your customer. In order to do that you have to go beyond the product. And your product should mirror the attitude and values you like to stand for. Mitsubishi stood for other values than Plymouth, and at that time these values were more important to the customer than the car itself.

You must constantly ask 'what reality are we talking about right now, real or perceived?' And then bear in mind that real reality has a tendency to come out on top, because it is so precise, even though you know that perceived reality is much more important. It is only by creating detailed documentation on how the brand is intended to be perceived and then making it available to everybody within the company, that perceived reality has a fair chance of measuring up to the real reality.

The importance of authenticity

DISNEY WORLD'S 'TOMORROW LAND' has now been recast as an historical artefact. Tradition is fashionable. Authenticity is increasingly a competitive advantage. Instead of inventing the future, companies are set on reinventing the past – some with more guile and commitment than others (witness the term 'genuine reproduction'). 'There is an increasing degree of fuzziness between what is real and what is fake,' observes John Naisbitt, author of *Megatrends* and *High Tech/High Touch*. 'The authenticity of a company's product or service is now all important. They need to establish intimacy with consumers.'

Some companies have already reintroduced people to answer their telephones rather than having automated systems. The cold mechanical hand of technology will only get you so far. The warm hand of humanity – the 'high touch' of Naisbitt's book's title – is required to maximize the business potential of technology. 'It is embracing technology that preserves our humanness and rejecting technology that intrudes upon it,' says Naisbitt.

In today's world of make-believe and cybermania, things you can believe in are becoming much more valuable. The substance a brand can produce in the form of a real and good story, a story about true passion, dedication, and commitment, is a compelling platform on which to build the future brand. Some branded companies, products, and services obviously have a hard time producing that kind of a story. But many have all they need, if only they are able to go back to their roots.

When Linus Torvalds began to write the most popular operating system for web servers – later branded Linux, as is the movement he started under that name – he did it for purely authentic reasons. He and his colleagues around the world were always looking for improvement, not in order to make money, but more idealistically – or practically – to give the world a better operating system. The freeware attitude created by the people in the Linux community has since influenced the Internet as a whole.

The Linux community is representative of the power of authenticity and the organic life force in human beings. They didn't let themselves be stopped by Microsoft's dominance and commercial attitude. On the contrary, it was the movement's greatest challenge.

This authenticity is not just about some fluffy idealism, making money or not. Quite the reverse. It has far more to do with doing things for their own sake than with anything else. 'A man has to do what a man has to do' is the background to such a phenomenon. And this pursuit of dedication, honesty, and idealism will be richly rewarded if it's a part of a Brand Code.

The challenge of Adidas

BLOOD, SWEAT AND TEARS, glory and defeat. That's what dedicated athletes around the world live with every day. The Adidas brand is synonymous with that struggle. In recent years the brand has won its own struggle, making an impressive comeback.

The brand of Olympic champions was initiated and nurtured by Adi Dassler, who began his business in Herzogenaurach, Germany, in the 1920s. In 1949 the Adidas (a compression of Adi and Dassler) company was officially registered along with the visual trademark of the brand – three white stripes.

Adi Dassler was passionate about sport. The archetypal sports fan made shoes that were like no one else's. They enclosed the athletes' feet like a second skin. Among his early fans was the legendary American athlete Jesse Owens, who won four gold medals and set five world records wearing Adi Dassler shoes.

Dassler was also a close follower and fan of the German national soccer team. For the 1954 World Cup final, he invented screw-in molded rubber studs that gave a firm grip. With Germany crowned as world champions, a lot of international media attention focused on the shoes with the white stripes. From then on, Adi Dassler was feted as 'the nation's greatest shoemaker.'

The greatest shoemaker created one of the greatest brands. Dassler's success can be attributed to a number of factors. First, Dassler had a driving ambition to make the best performing sport shoes. He continuously invented features that improved the sport shoes he produced so that the athletes could enhance their performance. Although he was a shoemaker at heart, a craftsman of sorts, there was something else that drove him. His relationship with the athletes was crucial. He won their trust and commitment to the Adidas brand.

When Dassler had an idea for improving an attribute of a shoe, or a new piece of equipment, he would go and talk to the athletes, about new techniques in training, what problems they might be facing. Whether he was talking to a football player, a fencing champion, or a discus thrower, Dassler continuously gathered feedback on his ideas. This constant communication helped create a trusting bond between him as a producer and them as professionals who depended on the best equipment for improved performance.

Dassler looked at one sport at a time. He became really involved in the particular traits of the athletes. This eventually made it possible for Adidas to reach a wide variety of sports and athletes – and, without any thought of strategy, to build a brand recognized throughout the world. The secret behind the company's success prior to the 1980s, according to Dassler, was purely and simply the core belief of sticking to producing high quality athletes' shoes and the commitment of its people to innovate and put attention to detail first.

Another central factor was communicating the adidas brand in an organized manner. It was Adi Dassler's son Horst Dassler who realized the potential the adidas brand had to reach around the world. At the 1956 Melbourne Olympics he sought out the fastest runners and strongest throwers, and gave them free adidas merchandise. In the next 30 years almost 75 per cent of Olympic medal winners wore Adidas shoes. They appeared in newspapers and newsreels, and showcased the three white stripes.

Horst Dassler cemented adidas's leadership position as a sports politician. He was an influential figure on the International Olympics Committee (IOC) and the international soccer body FIFA. He cared deeply about sports but also realized that times were changing. During the 1960s, the ethics of sports underwent a fundamental shift. Olympian ideals, sportsmanship, and fair play became a billion-dollar business and athletes demanded to be paid for wearing a specific brand.

As the world of sports changed, adidas started to face fierce competition from other brands, including American upstarts like Nike and the British company Reebok. Suddenly, adidas appeared old before its time. It seemed complacent, unable to adapt fast enough to new sporting trends, trends it was no longer driving. The focus of the brand became dissipated as it tried to do too many things simultaneously – becoming involved in everything from tennis wear to cross-country skis. Its products were inferior and technologically out of date compared with those of its competitors.

While Adidas continued to rely on its old shoe technology, Nike cleverly engineered high shock-absorption models, like 'Air,' just as the jogging boom took off. Negative images of adidas and falling consumer confidence negatively reinforced each other. Negatives multiplied. It became perceived as a 'boring' and 'everyday' brand, a brand that your dad would wear when he was washing the car on the driveway on a Sunday morning. Through the 1980s the competition tightened its grip. Nike marketed its athletes – as adidas had once done. Carl Lewis, sponsored by Nike, won four gold medals on home soil during the 1984 Los Angeles Olympics.

The Dassler family were, by then, struggling to run the company themselves. The downward spiral worsened as there was no strategic direction or major plan of where to go and what to focus on. Eventually, to ensure survival, the family sold the company to Bernard Tapie and the Tapie Finance Group. Tapie, a former football club owner in France, was famous for buying companies in trouble, dividing them into smaller parts and then selling them off.

Although Adidas lost ground, it did not entirely disappear from view. The original strength of the brand was such that a residue of awareness remained. In 1993, after a period of devastating results, the banks brought in Gilberte Beaux as CEO. The new management started by shaking up the company's marketing operation and restructuring into business units. New people were brought in and, in the short space of two years, the old organization was replaced by an entirely new one.

Research indicated that young consumers didn't care for the Adidas brand; they had no fascination with or attraction to it. Since this group represents the early adopters that often lead trends in the sporting goods market, this couldn't be ignored. The future of the brand looked bleak.

Enter Robert Louis-Dreyfus. He realized that the potential lay in the Adidas brand name and that the only way back was to reaffirm the company's original values. The future, Dreyfus realized, lay in rediscovering the high quality standards developed for a long time and built on German technology and innovative power, to harness the Adidas brand's reputation and the worldwide distribution network.

'We are going to care for our brand, and make sure not to lose focus,' Louis-Dreyfus declared. 'That's why our core business strategy is to make the best performance products for every sport – which we will show by being associated with some of the finest athletes around.'

For the first time, Adidas started to use strategic advertising in combination with event marketing in its marketing mix. The Adidas brand badly needed to rebuild credibility and awareness with a new generation of sports fans. To bond with the young target audience, the company had to adapt to new and more relevant sports that would appeal to this group. The Adidas management went to the US and brought back streetball, an alternative to traditional basketball, played outside on a concrete court. They created teams and a national tournament, involving kids everywhere. They also introduced a smaller-scale soccer tournament, the Predator's Cup, which has now become immensely popular.

But Adidas also started to pay close attention to new and emerging sports like BMX and skateboarding. This was a response to how young people view active participation in sports – very differently from previous generations – first and foremost because they want to have fun together. Scoring a goal or crossing the line first is secondary. In addition, they are looking for individual sports, where the experience and beauty of performance are more important.

Fortuitously, the hip-hop scene in New York adopted the Adidas symbol. Recognizing its good fortune, the company began to pick up on this emerging fashion statement, reproducing original Adidas products like the Stan Smith and Superstar shoe models.

The company deliberately set out to ride on the retro movement, although in a different setting, slowly succeeding in building an image among the young target audience as the 'trendy brand' of preference. Managers realized the danger of mass producing fashionable products. They had to keep the momentum and produce very selectively, using a very clear distribution strategy. One important move was the decision not to sell these products in sporting goods stores but in smaller trend shops. Had Adidas mass produced, most likely the trend would have faded and hurt the brand image in the long-term. What the management did was for the wellbeing of the brand rather than for the business. The success lay in authenticity; in this case young people themselves rediscovered and adapted the 'stripes.' The symbol was not forced on them by a marketing blitz.

Brand strength also needed to be regained among other groups. Part of the strategy has been to win ground in the US sporting-goods market, the largest in the world. But the sheer size of the US market meant strong worldwide influence for brands like Nike, with clear advantages from a stronghold on US home ground By connecting to US-type sports and athletes, Adidas's aim was to rebuild a worldwide image. It teamed up with the New York Yankees, with American colleges to outfit their football teams, and with NBA hero Kobe Bryant, and it became the official supplier to the women's soccer 1999 FIFA World Cup.

At the 1996 Atlanta Olympic games, Adidas equipped 6,000 athletes who won 229 medals – this success was followed by a 50 per cent increase in apparel sales. In 1998, the Adidas-sponsored French soccer team defeated the Brazilians, who coincidentally wore Nike. And for the year 2000 Olympic Games in Sydney, Adidas expected to outfit 26 out of 28 Olympic sports. Today, Adidas is number three in the US market.

FUNCTIONAL DIMENSION

It is still right to build on the old athletic tradition for the functional dimension. It is here that the brand has come back to build on the German engineering tradition of excellent equipment that helps the athlete and the everyday sports enthusiast perform better.

SPIRITUAL DIMENSION

The spiritual dimension is really a tribute to the sports tradition as a whole; Adidas has been part of something larger than simply producing sports shoes for athletes. As well as being involved with the Olympics and traditional sports, it has been an initiator. It has played an important role in bringing innovative and more 'up-to-date' sports to a large and younger audience.

MENTAL DIMENSION

Again, bringing to life deep-rooted values to dress them in something new and timely is what can make the mental perception of authenticity sound right to the new generation of sport fans.

Adidias Brand Mind Space

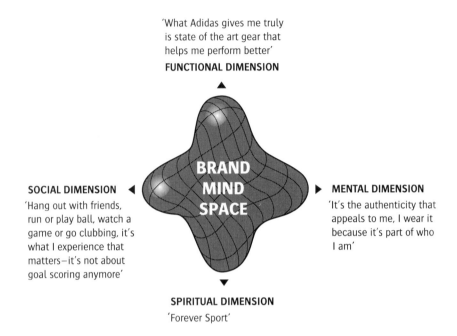

'What Adidas gives me truly is state of the art gear that helps me perform better'

FUNCTIONAL DIMENSION

SOCIAL DIMENSION

'Hang out with friends, run or play ball, watch a game or go clubbing, it's what I experience that matters—it's not about goal scoring anymore'

BRAND MIND SPACE

MENTAL DIMENSION

'It's the authenticity that appeals to me, I wear it because it's part of who I am'

SPIRITUAL DIMENSION

'Forever Sport'

SOCIAL DIMENSION

The social dimension is perhaps the strongest of all. If the perception of the brand can have a wider reach than merely being an identification tool in relation to others, it has the ability to attract the audience more strongly. The cult that has formed around the Adidas brand is strong among a young audience that cares about sport and the 'experience' of it, about taking part rather than winning, about overall performance rather than just scoring goals.

A company and brand require more than just the right people. A brand needs direction, it needs to have fundamental values to build on and a vision and strategy to grow the organization into the future. Robert Louis-Dreyfus said about taking on the Adidas brand and company: 'The brand name and its history is the greatest capital to rebuild the Adidas company upon.'

"All the world's a stage,
And all the men and women merely players.
They have their exits and their entrances,
And one man in his time plays many parts,
His acts being seven ages."

William Shakespeare, *As You Like It*

CREATING A 4-D BRAND

Understanding transparency

THE ROUTE TO the transparent market has taken us through three distinct stages: product marketing, niche marketing, and the rise of the critical consumer.

PRODUCT MARKETING

In the immediate postwar years, the mass market, driven by an ambition to cross social barriers, ruled the corporate roost. This resulted in a very class-focused approach to marketing. It was true product-based marketing built on mass production and standardized products. The sole emphasis was on product differentiation. The brand guaranteed the quality of the product. Production values were the key drivers.

NICHE MARKETING

In the 1970s, niche marketing was introduced. The driver was social imitation, resulting in a lifestyle approach. The basis for this was customer segmentation and niche production. The notion of lifestyle focused on consumer differences. Within this, the role of the brand was to add value to the physical product. The production origin was hidden from the consumer, and the focus was totally on the concept or lifestyle. Niche marketing was also façade marketing.

MARKETING TO THE CRITICAL CONSUMER

At the end of the twentieth century marketing underwent a paradigm shift, in an attempt to create a more basic proposition, focusing on situation and function. Better informed than ever before – a process accelerated by the Internet – new consumers are much more critical than their predecessors. The consumer is the ultimate expert. The consumer penetrates the façade and reveals what is behind it, simply by asking a lot of difficult questions about such matters as production ethics and the origin of products. The consumer also puts pressure on the brand value, questioning the price premium, and is generally looking for 'real' value. Many basic criteria are taken for granted, including ecological responsibility, production ethics, safety, and quality. Question them.

THE TRANSPARENT MARKET

The advent of the transparent market has important implications for branding. The openness created by the Internet makes this development more dramatic. Production is now controlled by customer values – the needs of the individual are the dominant driver. The result is transparent production where the customer has full insight, and products that are also transparent, including the values and the knowledge behind them. Everything becomes open to the consumer.

In the new transparent market, companies must decide on their role. In the traditional market, many companies managed to play hide and seek and maintain several different roles at the same time for different audiences, sometimes being suppliers, sometimes distributing in their own name, and sometimes being just a knowhow partner. Since consumers found it hard to penetrate this, it was never really a problem. In the web-driven transparent market of today, such a situation is no longer tenable. (A number of well-known brands have found themselves in difficulties because they did not adjust to the change fast enough. Look at how UPS stole a march on FedEx.)

In response to this change, every company needs to sit down and review its strategies to find out what role it should play in the market. In the transparent market there are two main roles:

PRODUCTION BRAND

A production brand focuses totally on its production. The technology and expertise manifested in patents, methods, and unique know-how become the brand's most important asset. Production decides what is possible, what is feasible, and what is cost efficient. A production brand is not locked into a single customer relationship. It has to sell to everyone and its goal is to be the best in its category.

This is not like the big industrial companies of the past controlling distribution to the end customer. Today's production brands have to rely on partnerships and their marketing tools include *ingredient branding* (witness Gore-Tex, Intel, and Nutrasweet) and *co-branding* (witness Coca-Cola and McDonald's). You can also find production brands among service businesses, such as the security company Securitas, branding itself openly when serving, for instance, a bank or a shopping mall.

RELATION BRAND

A relation brand is totally relation/situation focused. The brand's most important asset is its unique platform (such as a distribution system) and the knowledge it has about the behaviour and needs of its customers. And, in the same way that a production brand can't afford to be locked into one distributor, a relation brand can't afford to be locked into a single production chain.

Typical of a relation brand is IKEA, with its family concept. Its strength lies in knowing its customers better than anyone in its business. Typically for a relation brand, it can satisfy the needs of its customers only by being able to choose production sources freely.

Dell is another very good example of a relation brand doing the same thing; paying full attention to the needs and preferences of the customer. In the relation brand world the customer decides. Many New Economy brands could also fit into this category, particularly those that provide a delivery mechanism or shop window.

In this new context an 'ecosystem of needs' has to be created in which production and relation brands interact. The forms of these ecosystems of needs are going to develop rapidly over next few years. For relation brands it is useful to think in terms of meeting places – a portal on the Web is such a meeting place. For production brands, thinking in terms of ingredient branding is important; you are not just an anonymous supplier, but a brand in the mind of the customer adding value to the relation brand.

The consumer role-play

LEADING RESEARCHERS IN consumer behaviour state that some consumption can be explained by 'role theory.' All of us perceive ourselves to be a little different; we don't see ourselves as the same as everyone else. This perception can either be positive or negative. Interestingly, the consumption of high-interest products, such as cars, is very much the result of the customer's desire to be someone that he or she is not. Consumers choose brands according to how well they fit with their desired perception and the brand's ability to communicate this.

Consumers use brands in the same way as actors use theatrical props to augment and clarify their role and personality.

There are several global 'roles' with which people want to be associated. And for each role there is a set of appropriate brands helping the consumer to show their desired belonging.

One example is the traditional English country style. These consumers are supposed to drive a Jaguar or a Range Rover, wear a Barbour jacket, arrange weekend hunts, own a Labrador, and so on. Another example is the surf culture, with its symbolic worldwide brands. Surfers wear Billabong clothes and wetsuits, surf on Quicksilver boards, and carry their boards around in a DaKine board bag. People put together a personal mix of certain brands to feel like individuals, but at the same time they stick to the 'right' brands in order to belong to the group. This is the best of both worlds.

People play different roles in different situations. The rebellious, individualistic surf dude behaves differently when he is out shopping with his mother. We behave differently at work than we do at home. A single consumer may have multiple behaviours depending on which role is appropriate at that moment. The most important criteria when choosing a brand are not static; rather, they depend on the situation.

High-interest products don't have to be very expensive ones. Every brand that is perceived to enhance self-perception is interesting. Because of this, there is huge market potential for even traditional, uninteresting, and boring products that can fit into this category. Products that are more based on routine purchase and consumption, like milk or toilet paper, can be developed into interesting brands. It doesn't have to be a purely utilitarian brand. If the brand stands for something that touches the consumer, then it will attain a tighter relationship with the consumer.

One company that exemplifies this is the New Pig Corporation. Industrial clean-up is a dirty business but someone has to do it. And no one does it quite like New Pig. From its headquarters in Pork Avenue, Tipton, Pennsylvania, the company has built a $70 million direct marketing business from making and selling absorbent products to mop up leaks and spills. You don't need a degree from Insead or Harvard Business School to understand New Pig. There is, the company cheerfully admits, nothing particularly clever or strategic about its brand or its business formula. It takes unglamorous but useful products and adds some hoggy humor. In the process, New Pig has created a distinctive brand – and a unique business culture.

New Pig grew out of an industrial cleaning firm, and claims to have put the 'contained absorbents industry' on the map. Frustrated with the traditional low-tech approach to oil and grease spills – spreading loose clay around the base of leaky machinery – founders Don Beaver and Ben Stapelfield experimented with alternative solutions. In 1985, the duo invented the 'Pig Absorbent Sock,' a nylon sock filled with an absorbent powder. Their new creation was as happy wallowing around in muck as its porcine namesake. That gave them the idea for the company.

A clever blend of quality products and piggy branding has been bringing home the bacon ever since. It has transformed what might otherwise have been a bland industrial cleaning firm into a marketing phenomenon. Take a typical New Pig product – an absorbent mat that can be put around a machine to soak up spills. In New Pig's capable trotters, it becomes the altogether more interesting Ham-O Pig Mat – complete with a colourful piggy pattern and slogan ('tough as a pig's hide'), and a cartoon pig dressed in overalls.

'There's not a market in the world where people don't like to laugh and have fun and be treated as important customers,' observes Stapelfield. Between 1985 and 1989, sales of New Pig's industrial mop-up products grew by almost 4,000 per cent, and by 1990, New Pig ranked as one of the top 100 fastest-growing small firms in the US.

In the (admittedly more exotic) market for ice-cream, Ben & Jerry's is another case in point. The company that gave the world ice-cream flavours like Cherry Garcia (after Grateful Dead guitarist Jerry Garcia), Chubby Hubby, and Chunky Monkey has always had a serious side. Its founders Ben Cohen and Jerry Greenfield believe that business has a responsibility to act as an agent of social change. The company donates 7.5 per cent of its annual pretax profits to social causes. Its hippie ideals and social agenda make it stand out. In a business world where most companies march to the same drum, any company that boogies to a different beat is bound to attract attention.

Personal values seem to have a very strong influence on people's consumption. Basic values are developed up to the age of 25 and kept for the rest our lives unless something very dramatic occurs. It is therefore possible to have a glimpse of the ruling values of tomorrow just by studying values of young people today. These are going to influence the possibilities for brands in the future. Coca-Cola has experienced this in the last couple of years. Because of changing values among young people, Pepsi has been able to attract drinkers with a new type of message. Coca-Cola has traditionally built its brand on social values, while Pepsi lately has chosen a brand message aimed more at the individual.

What does all this tell us about consumers and why they buy brands? It tells us that brands exist primarily – if not entirely – in the minds of consumers. Brands are all about perception. What really matters for a brand is that it connects with its target audience. As Mike Clasper of Procter & Gamble puts it, what really matters is 'share of mind, rather than share of shelf.'

Discovering new dimensions

WHEN I LEFT my job in the advertising business in 1997 and started out in my new profession as brand consultant, I began by studying the most successful brands I could think of. Role modelling is always a good way to learn. I was curious to find out if there might be a pattern of some sort in the behaviour of the branding masters. Read the history of some of these companies and you will find many coincidences leading to their eventual success. Just as it is for everyone in life, the best things are seldom planned.

I wanted to find a way to influence the destiny of a brand by some kind of structured thinking. My ambition was to start the branding process in a systematic, yet simple way, by describing from the customer and market point of view what would be the drivers for liking (or disliking) a brand.

I also wanted to be able to measure and target the *perception* of the brand in the *mind* of the *customer*, or prospective customer – to be able to map out graphically what I choose to call the Brand Mind Space of a particular brand and develop it verbally in the form of ideal expected customer statements. I had seen a lot of consumer research of a similar kind during my advertising years, but it seemed complicated and difficult to use in practical brand-building work.

I began clustering all the different things that helped the best brands succeed (and, in some cases what they didn't do, but their competitors did instead). After a while, I found out that building a brand in the consumer's mind always seemed to fall into four different categories, or 'dimensions' as I prefer to call them. These are the basis for the 4-D Branding model.

THE FUNCTIONAL DIMENSION

The first of these four dimensions – the *functional dimension* – was pretty simple to track down. Almost always, the need to build a brand starts with making a more or less unique product or service, and the benefit for the customer is the basis for the brand. That is the perceived benefit, not necessarily the real benefit that the inventor or the engineer had in mind, but the one actually experienced by the customer.

In the moment of invention the need for a name to label the new product arises. There is a Chinese proverb 'without a name a thing doesn't exist,' which of course is true. It is especially true when you want to convince somebody else, so you need a name quickly. Most innovators feel that the more intriguing the name is, the better the new invention will be perceived. This may well be correct, but sometimes the need to have a name becomes overly desperate and it is chosen so quickly that there is no time

Brand Mind Space™

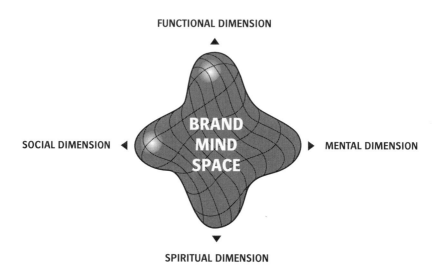

For example, when Nike named its patented air-cushioned shoe technology 'Nike *air*,' the name refers to the breathing of the runner as well as the lightness of the shoe, and consequently the runner's step. It also describes the patented air technology itself. Some of us still remember how athletic shoes were before Nike – flat and static, leaving aching heels and strained, heavy legs – so we know how good Nike's clever sub-brand was.

The *functional* dimension describes the perceived benefit of the products or services connected with the brand. And that is where everything used to start in the old days. In the 1950s, the perceived benefit of the product was all that was communicated about the brand. The development from communicating the actual benefit to the benefit perceived by the customer was a great step in advertising.

The *functional* dimension is still very important in modern marketing in many business areas. Everything that has to do with physical quality, taste, style *per se*, and efficiency falls into the functional category. The importance of the *functional* dimension also depends on where in its lifecycle the brand is. The earlier in the lifecycle, the more important the functional attributes are to define the brand's justification, role, and sometimes the physical benefit.

All brand builders who depend heavily on the *functional* dimension sooner or later face the problem of diminishing difference. The competitor is closing in on the functional dimension. In the service sector this can happen overnight, since services are often openly produced interactively with the customer and are usually very easy to copy. In high-tech markets product lifecycles are also very short. When the threat of being copied looms large, every brand builder tends to look for areas in which they can create something unique.

THE SOCIAL DIMENSION

What then enters the brand-builder's mind is the *social* dimension, since social life and social acceptance are so important. In his Meta-Management theory, Swedish business thinker Carl Eric Linn makes a new attempt to explain branding from a biological perspective, reconstructing the classical Maslow pyramid of human needs. On top of his pyramid Linn has *mating*, securing the survival of the species. Courting, fighting, and seduction are all part of the mating ritual. This has little to do with sexuality in today's culture, it is basic programming, a pattern that we tend to follow instinctively. Leading to *mating* is *social identity*, or the need to be socially accepted by the group and by its leading members. Buyers in any market make their purchase decision subjectively, basing it on what they feel best conveys or portrays their social identity.

With growing instability in society, brands appear to take over as identifications. The traditional class society is dying, and instead we are moving to a kind of 'branding society.' In the *social* dimension the brand quite often creates a cult around itself, it becomes a social insignia, or a 'prop' in the lifestyle play of an individual.

In the *social* dimension the trademark, or the logo, itself becomes the symbol of the cult society that a brand ideally creates, very much like the flag of a country. Think of the eagle wings of Harley-Davidson, or, again, Nike with its famous swoosh. The carrier of the symbol is easily identified and appreciated openly or silently by other members of this cult society. If you see someone running with the same brand on their vest as you have or someone stepping out of the same car as you have, you feel there is a bond – however sad this may be. (This also works in reverse. We can form an instant dislike of someone based purely on their brand choices.)

The drive to feel we are among friends is very strong not only for consumers, but equally for business-to-business customers. The social dimension plays an important part in the choice of, for instance, management consultants. A brand like McKinsey is very strong on this dimension. For most top managers, joining the McKinsey customer club is almost the definition of leadership. Hiring McKinsey can actually boost a company's stock price.

IBM used to cultivate the expression 'It's never wrong to buy an IBM.' 'No one ever got fired for buying IBM' was another slogan, and for many years (and maybe even still) the *social* dimension has been the most important component in the IBM brand. This aspect is much more important than the *functional* dimension, where many of its competitors offer better or equally good products or solutions.

THE MENTAL DIMENSION

The social dimension very much reflects the relationship between customers and a group of people to which they want to belong. The brand is a valuable tool of identification in front of others. At the other end of the same axis is what I call the *mental* dimension. This has little to do with what other people think of you, and all to do with what you think of yourself. The best brands are not only strong on the *social* dimension, they are also strong on the *mental* side. This dimension is by its nature a much more profound dimension: it really penetrates deep inside your personality. Here the brand touches what most of as would call our soul. In every human being there is an inner landscape of mental programming.

The *mental dimension* is about personal transformation. It's about change and getting new insights about yourself. If someone had told me ten years ago that brands would have this effect on people I would have laughed in disbelief. But the truth is that some of the best brands of the future will fulfil the role of a personal coach facilitating mental change. They will in some cases substitute for the kind of mentor traditionally found among more senior friends and colleagues.

All individuals need to have role models on which to model their life and behaviour. The brand and its mental dimension serve that purpose. Experiences from early childhood up to the present day largely set our personalities, reaction and behaviour. Sometimes this results in low self-esteem in certain areas of life. Help with *reframing* these mental pictures of ourselves is very important to us, and therefore a great opportunity for a brand builder. Some of the problems we have with our mental pictures are very individual and hard to make general. But a lot of our reframing is shared with most of our fellow humans. One of them is the excuses we use in order to avoid certain unpleasant or demanding activities.

That's why the Nike expression 'Just do it' is so effective. It travels straight to our conscious mind, and reminds us how important it is to overcome that feeling of avoidance or passivity. Of course, for any athlete – professional or amateur – this is a highly relevant expression; the only way to prove how good you are is to 'just do it.' It doesn't matter how much you think you could do in theory (if you really wanted), you just have to prove it.

BMW obviously has a very strong social dimension, being a status car, but it shares that with many others, like Mercedes and Audi. What distinguishes BMW from the other car brands is its strong mental dimension, which in today's car market proves to be extremely valuable to get the higher margins that produce profit. The *mental* dimension of BMW is in German 'freude am fahren,' in English 'the joy of driving,' a very personal experience.

Another example of efficiency in *social* as well as *mental* dimensions is Marlboro with its 'lonely cowboy'. The *social* dimension might be the more obvious of the two, the identification with the group of 'real men' personalized by the cowboy. But the *mental* dimension of Marlboro is an equally powerful tool for individuals to mentally role model, or handle, the feeling of loneliness and alienation so common among urban citizens.

The personal pleasure, or kick, we get out of owning something special is very important in brand building, and this is the way most exclusive brands start their career. In my office I have a Charles Eames chair made out of steel and black leather. It's a classic chair, and I have an original. Most visitors who see my chair don't know it's an original and expensive Charles Eames chair. Most of them don't even know about the famous American architect and furniture designer. And to most of them the chair looks very cold and uncomfortable. So having this chair is not really of any use for my social identification. But the *mental* dimension of this chair is enormous for me. Every time I sit in my chair I feel this little kick; it doesn't matter if nobody else understand its qualities, because I do.

When a small and fairly unknown clock manufacturer in a valley in Switzerland – Breitling – became a brand it was first on a *mental* dimension. Breitling is traditionally a special aviator's watch. People bought a Breitling watch to feel special. For anyone who regarded Rolex as being the socially most accepted brand to carry on your wrist, the Breitling brand initially offered little *social* dimension. Now Breitling has even built strength on that dimension. It has become a real cult brand among certain groups of people, for whom Breitling has become one of the most important lifestyle properties.

The safety element in Volvo's brand is another example of how well the *mental* dimension in a brand can satisfy an individual's need for security, comfort, and peace of mind.

When IKEA's Swedish ad campaign proclaimed 'Not for the rich, but for the clever', it was using the mental dimension to negate its more exclusive competitors. Who wants to be rich and stupid?

The brand 'Intel Inside' is a good example of a strong mental dimension. Compared with the dominance of the social safety of buying an IBM (although there is a *mental* component as well here, the feeling of personal safety and comfort), the Intel Inside has a much stronger mental effect. Its label on my business computer gives me an everyday reminder about the power and the 'intelligence' that Intel provides me with as an individual in my work. This secret ingredient of my computer has become almost a personal guarantee for success.

Some brands also cleverly satisfy our personal need for being modern and 'with-it'. Sony gives you this feeling in the high-tech area. Boss does it in men's fashion and Gucci in women's fashion, for instance. The price premium we pay for fashion brands is not only based on the *social* dimension but equally the *mental* dimension.

THE SPIRITUAL DIMENSION

The spiritual dimension sounds somewhat religious. (In Sweden in particular many people are suspicious of matters religious so I sometimes use the word idealistic instead.) Spiritual refers to the larger system of which we are all a part. Understand the spiritual and you understand the connections between the brand, the product or the company, and the bigger system.

In the period just after the Industrial Revolution (in Sweden, for example, this is the late nineteenth century; in the UK it goes back further), the patriarchs of industry often embodied a very strong, self-assumed spiritual or ethical dimension in building their enterprises. Industrial barons shouldered the responsibility for their workers. Society was still unable to offer any form of social security, and almost all cultural sponsorship came from the pockets of the newly rich industrialists. In most western countries, especially in Scandinavia and Europe, this has changed dramatically. Society has now taken over the dominant responsibility for welfare, infrastructure, and cultural development, as well as environmental issues.

What we have seen in the last ten years is a backlash toward a more enterprise-dependent system. What is genuinely new about the spiritual, or the ethical, dimension is the fact that it is now purposely used to build brands. The problem with this is that you cannot be just a little ethical.

Brands that set themselves up as paragons in this area lay themselves open to criticism if they don't live up to the high standards they preach.

As Jerry Greenfield, co-founder of Ben & Jerry's, has observed, 'When you're outspoken and vocal about having high ideals, you set yourself up for criticism and you will be criticized. You want to be held to high standards. The danger is that you start getting gun shy. That's the worst thing you can do.'

If you start on this path, you have to follow it through, as both the Body Shop and Ben & Jerry's have tried to do. (This has not protected either from regular attacks in the media, however.) In fact, the Body Shop is one of the best examples of a brand created almost entirely on the spiritual dimension. When Anita Roddick started the company the cosmetic branding market was firmly rooted in the social and mental dimensions.

To be beautiful in front of others, to have movie stars and supermodels as role models, is a very typical social dimension. To feel fresh, attractive and young at heart is a very typical mental dimension. Very little of the functional dimension was in the brand perception of most cosmetic brands. The traditional cosmetics customer didn't really care what worked in a functional sense. Maybe no one had asserted or proved that this was relevant. Anita Roddick, however, claimed that the modern working woman is far from uninterested in the functional aspect of cosmetics. On the contrary, they will not spend time using something that is not efficient, nor do they like to expose their bodies to something that is not healthy.

But it was on the spiritual dimension that Anita Roddick created a real difference between the Body Shop brand and everybody else. She stated that her cosmetics were not tested on animals, she dramatized it and made the case with such passion that it soon became the clearest signal of the Body Shop. She actually created her own window of opportunity and monopolized the non-animal-tested cosmetics market.

The cosmetics business in general continued to maintain that animal testing was a necessity to avoid serious customer allergy problems. At first it probably thought that Anita Roddick's brand message was both stupid and unnecessary; this, of course, is a typical sign of a brand being different. But Roddick established the brand by persisting in her message, later expanding the spiritual dimension to include a wider ethical view on environmental issues as well as a respect for communities in developing countries. More recently, the mental dimension has been developed with aromatherapy, which is typically addressed to the customer's personal wellbeing. On the social dimension the Body Shop has created a sort of virtual community mainly comprised of women who support what it stands for.

One brand, many Brand Mind Spaces™

THE FOUR DIMENSIONS – functional, social, mental and spiritual – provide the basis for understanding the true nature and future potential of a brand. No brand exists just in one dimension. The hard part is mapping out the overlap between dimensions. What I call the Brand Mind Space is a way of representing the brand in all four areas. You can think of it as a figure drawn on four axes. Simply, it is the shape of the brand in all four dimensions.

So, for example, the BMW brand is high on the functional axis, high on the mental axis, and high on the social axis. Its weakness lies in the spiritual dimension, where it is low. This suggests that brand managers in Munich should think hard about how they could increase the brand's spiritual depth – without damaging it on the other three dimensions. The simple, but logical, message would be to link future designs to environmental issues, or other causes that are near to consumers' hearts.

In reality, every individual customer has an individual Brand Mind Space. But in strategic brand work this is impractical. Usually I cluster one, two, or maybe three groups together: for instance the end-users, the retailers, or the alliance partners. Or it could be the stakeholders of the brand, the customers, the employees, the owners, and public opinion. All of these groups would have a different interpretation of the brand.

The brand cannot adapt to all these different interest groups; it is not a chameleon. The aim is to create a very well-defined, distinct brand. In order to do that we need give the brand one very clear coding, and that is the next phase in our process. When creating that code we use one, or several, Brand Mind Spaces as a diagnostic tool to identify new activities or spin-offs, but also as a check to test them against.

It is vital to take the next step carefully. Hasty conclusions can cause disastrous mistakes. In 1985 Coca-Cola, for example, announced to the world that it was replacing its traditional recipe cola with New Coke. In detailed research it had discovered that the new recipe was preferred by most consumers. It was, they said, smoother, sweeter, and preferable to the old version. The decision was based on the functional dimension alone. It ignored the social and mental dimensions of the brand. The old version was selling in many millions every day of the week, and was much loved by consumers. Coke was faced with a torrent of criticism. On the other hand, its arch-rival Pepsi could barely contain its glee – indeed, it quickly produced advertising that rubbed in the fact that 'the real thing' remained unchanged. Realizing that its move had been disastrous, Coke backtracked and, after 90 days, reintroduced the original coke. The recipe has not been tinkered with since.

In Europe, Monsanto made a similar mistake. When it looked at the future of genetically modified foods, the company considered the functional dimension, and was blind to the spiritual dimension. It set about building its brand on the basis of the functional benefits. The scientific arguments were generally accepted in the US, but this positioning ran into problems in Europe, where there was an emotional backlash. Had Monsanto developed the spiritual dimension of its brand in advance, it might have been better prepared to weather the storm. Had it achieved greater understanding of its commitment to, and respect for, placing humanity above science, it would have had a better foundation on which to build.

As these two examples demonstrate, the key to success lies in understanding how the brand and its essence – the Brand Code – will perform in different scenarios. Futurizing the brand depends on creating a code that is both robust and sufficiently flexible to allow it to adjust to changing circumstances. If a brand comes under attack, it is in a better position to respond if it can bolster its appeal on more than one dimension. By developing the Brand Code, a company can obtain a clear view of how its brand might be interpreted by the consumers of the future. That code then becomes the critical management tool to drive the organization.

The stage character – The Brand Code™

THE BRAND CODE aims to encapsulate the future positioning of the brand. It answers the question: What should this company really be about? It involves working through a series of possible scenarios to gain an understanding of how the brand might play to its various audiences. The Brand Code is the character that the brand could play on stage. It is not the actor, it is the role the actor has to play. The actors can be anybody from a salesperson to a receptionist to the art director at an advertising agency. The actor's job is all about interpreting the role and the character and bringing it to life, making it convincing and believable.

Needless to say, many interpretations are possible and also encouraged. In order to be able to utilize the creativity and personal talents of your people, it is important to give them a great deal of freedom in interpreting the Brand Code. But in order to make the brand consistent and homogeneous for the audience, it is important to ensure that the Brand Code is precise and well defined.

The purpose of the Brand Code is to create a future-driven brand, and the code is the central tool for doing that. The Brand Code extracts your company's DNA code, or that for your product or service. Everything will be derived or tuned in from this code. It is the very core of your company. It is the most important instrument in all kinds of decision making. It is not only convenient in the decision process always to back up your decisions by reference to the code, it is also necessary in order to build a strong, well-defined, and successful brand rapidly. The consistent branding approach that a brand-driven company takes to everything, on an everyday basis, is actually the most important secret of its success.

The Brand Code is a statement of what your company or your product stands for. It tells a story about your company. It is the business idea, the positioning, the vision and mission, and the values all in one package.

The Brand Code model resembles a spider and consists of six parts, or backgrounds, as well as a synthesis of them. These are:

> Product/Benefit
> Positioning
> Style
> Mission
> Vision
> Values

The Brand Code can be a few key words or a short sentence. Sometimes it is tempting to use the code in your communication as a tag line or generic (like 'Connecting People' for Nokia). But I usually recommend that my clients use the Brand Code as the mantra of the company; something that is internal, not used outside, but a secret weapon to guide everybody in everyday situations.

The first three of the six parts of the Brand Code are rooted in the present situation of the brand in its marketplace. The following three are the 'tomorrow' aspects of the brand, driving the brand dynamically into the future.

PRODUCT/BENEFIT

A carefully phrased description of the benefits the customer experiences in the deliverables of the company, the product, service, knowledge, and so on. This can be an easy task in most cases, but sometimes it takes a little work to get beyond the clichés of your business to find the bottom-line offer that you present to your customers. The benefit is closely related to the functional dimension.

The Brand Code™
The Definition of the Brand

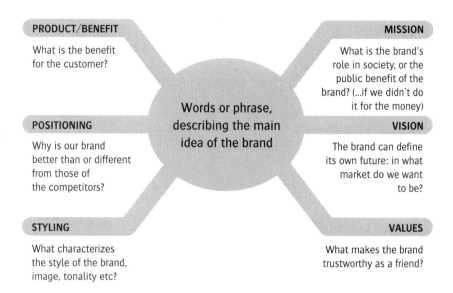

PRODUCT/BENEFIT

What is the benefit
for the customer?

POSITIONING

Why is our brand
better than or different
from those of
the competitors?

STYLING

What characterizes
the style of the brand,
image, tonality etc?

Words or phrase,
describing the main
idea of the brand

MISSION

What is the brand's
role in society, or the
public benefit of the
brand? (...if we didn't do
it for the money)

VISION

The brand can define
its own future: in what
market do we want
to be?

VALUES

What makes the brand
trustworthy as a friend?

POSITIONING

This is your response to the classic business positioning question – why
are you better than and/or different from your competitors? Remember
that the brand is the differentiation code of your company. Here we begin
to clinch our capabilities to create a difference. Usually this includes the
competence of doing something very well for a specific target audience.
You might also have competencies in your company that are not necessarily
as yet communicated in the benefit you deliver to your customers. The
positioning element in the Brand Code spins off the functional dimension.

STYLE

This describes the personal traits, image, attitude, and behaviour of the
brand, which can of course be a company or a product. I used also to call
it personality, meaning that part of the personal appearance that immediately meets the eye. The style is heavily influenced by the social dimension.

MISSION

In finding the mission for a company, product, or service, one has to go
beyond the benefit for the customer to explore the role in society, not

SAS Brand Code

PRODUCT/BENEFIT		MISSION
Airline service to-from-within Scandinavia		To celebrate and stimulate Scandinavian culture and business life

Simplicity
Freedom of Choice
Well-being

POSITIONING		VISION
For frequent travellers a reliable world-wide network		All Scandinavians should be proud of their airline

STYLING		VALUES
Equality Consideration Modesty Reliability Rationality Honesty		Is reliable Is business-like Is progressive Cares

necessarily globally but perhaps locally. The perspective should be longer and wider than is usually the case when traditionally using the expression mission. A good question to ask yourself is: What would we do if we didn't do it for the money?

For most companies recruiting young talent in competitive markets, this is a crucial part of the Brand Code. Young people in particular ask for a meaningful job, and this is equally or more important than the compensation. And companies that are not able to explain what contribution they make to society at large may not be on the short list of prospective workplaces for such people.

The mission is also very useful for directing public relations activities. It is strongly inspired by the spiritual dimension. In fact, the mission often turns the brand from a consumer brand into a stakeholder brand by giving the company the capacity for a higher pursuit.

The mission of Michelin, for example, is to promote (and rate) gourmet cuisine and ambience in accommodation. This is a very interesting mission for a tyre company. Needless to say, the Michelin Guides have given the company much more PR than the tyre business itself would have produced. (As a result, the guides are being spun off as a separate business under the title 'Guide Rouge.' Such is the strength of association, it is likely that the Michelin name will still be used by most consumers.)

VISION

The word vision has many definitions and is used in very different ways in management strategy. I use it in a very pragmatic way. Vision in the Brand Code is the positioning for the future – in what market do we want to be?

Quite often you have to create your own market. A typical example of this is when Rollerblades created the market for in-line skating. This also avoided the degeneration of its brand (think of what happened to Xerox, Vespa, and Thermos).

If you study some of the most successful brands, you will find that they have clear visions, which encompass not only their future marketplace but also what offerings they wish to provide, to whom, and usually when. (The timing is not necessary since timing it is difficult and less important for the brand, but more important in a business plan.) The vision is the most dynamic input to the Brand Code and in our workshops we put a great deal of emphasis on it.

VALUES

Last but not least come the values. I usually describe corporate values as rules of life. Sometimes you meet people who have very strong rules to live by, and this is impressive, no matter how peculiar these rules might be. Values emphasize the trustworthiness of the brand, the long-term personality that guarantees continuity, as values do in a personal friendship.

Though they are mainly non-verbal, the keywords attached to your values are important and should be chosen with care. A favourite word like 'honesty' is easy to put in without commitment, but imagine a worst-case scenario for your business and ask how much you would, without hesitating, let it cost you to be 'honest' – $50 million? $100 million? $200 million? Important as it is to have ethical words to drive your company, it can be dangerous if you are caught by journalists, customers, or competitors not living up to your own ethics. Take the personal values of your people as the staring point.

In entrepreneurial businesses, the values of the founder are usually set as corporate values. This makes them far more genuine than a contrived corporate strategy. When you work out your values it often leads to a discussion about whether a specific word is a value or a style. A style is something you will easily notice on your first encounter with a company. A value may take a while to experience. It is a long-term feature and therefore one might need to know your company, to use your products or services, for some time to tell. Values are also more philosophical in nature.

In addition to these six elements, I sometimes add two more. To clarify relationships between the brand and its various audiences and constituencies I look at stakeholders. I also examine structure to determine whether a brand is an ingredient brand or a master brands with several sub-brands.

Once you are satisfied with all your inputs consider what, in a few words, would help you to truly differentiate your company, product or service? What would create it in someone's mind? Synthesize all the elements.

The more freely you can think the better. You might end up with one, two, or three possibilities, but you will feel that one is stronger, and that might be the right one. Test your best one against all the six elements. If it is connected to, and gets support from, at least two or three of the parts, then you'll be OK. Check also that it doesn't conflict seriously with the rest of the parts. Verify that you will be able to use the Brand Code as a tool to drive your company. Are you able to set an attitude, to inspire and make decisions with it? Does your Code also contain a future drive? If so, you probably have the right one. Give it some time to establish itself. This often requires a couple of weeks. Pick it up and look at it a few times during this period.

The best Code doesn't make people super-enthusiastic at first. The best ones grow with time; and grow your brand.

5

"Whatever you can do,
or dream you can do, begin it.
Boldness has genius and power
and magic in it. Begin it now!"

Goethe

LIVING THE
4-D BRAND

Evangelizing the brand

GREAT IDEAS ARE just the start – strategizing without practice is an empty experience. You have to live your brand to be successful. Living the brand is hard work. Living the brand is personal. No one can implement a brand from a distance. No one can simply direct implementation. Like the successful entrepreneur, living the brand requires role modelling, symbolic management, a lot of passion, dedication, and a large amount of craziness. 'You've got to evangelize the concept,' says John Chambers, CEO of Cisco.

Building a new brand or modernizing an old one is like changing an operating system in your computer. The important difference is that it involves people, not just bits and bytes, so it is personal. An alternative view is that we are more programmed than we sometimes like to admit. We are programmed from early childhood through our relationship to our parents and to our brothers and sisters. We are also programmed by our schools and by our friends and experience. Later, in the world of work, we are programmed in the organization or corporation we work for and in the business we are in.

Much of this programming is quite useful and important; without it we wouldn't be able to do our jobs. But some of the programmes we run are full of bugs. They include distorted perceptions, and attitudes that are completely wrong and misplaced in a new business environment. Some of these malfunctions actually put not only the organization but our professional careers in danger. Many people find themselves out of a job because they fail to adapt to the new realities. Their companies or they themselves have not been able to get the latest updated versions of the operating system. (We go on to explore how 4-D Branding can be used by individuals to create new personal brands.)

Dr Richard Bandler, one of the founders of Neuro Linguistic Programming (NLP), used the analogy of programming when he introduced his methodology, which has since been used by trainers and psychoanalysts worldwide. NLP is an excellent approach to changing or breaking old patterns and turning people (and organizations) into something new, more productive, and future driven. Some people have ethical qualms about NLP.

It may appear manipulative, but good and popular leaders have always practised NLP. The difference is that we are now trying to put it into a system, so that the management team in a corporation will be able to use this knowledge in a more structured way, resulting in the entire organization living the brand.

Developing a new Brand Code involves breaking old patterns, as the market, or the environment, is changing. To do something new it is necessary to stop doing what you have been doing. A new Brand Code needs to move you ahead of the pack. Again, there are similarities with the entrepreneur who intuitively knows exactly how to programme, or reprogramme, employees with the right mental images, using the right language. Using the right kind of language makes the brain do the 'right' things instead of persisting with doing the wrong things.

Who should be responsible for the brand?

TRADITIONALLY, RESPONSIBILITY for the brand was delegated to the marketing department. Branding was perceived to be solely a marketing issue. Corporations with many brands, such as Procter & Gamble, have traditionally given substantial everyday responsibility for a brand to fairly junior staff. In many other companies, the actual responsibility for a brand has remained unclear.

In highly successful companies where the brand is the core of the business, top management regards the brand as the most important management tool. So top management – the CEO, the board of directors – should be in charge of a company's brand. After all, what else is there to be in charge of?

At the same time, establishing a company's Brand Code requires the involvement and commitment of both the formal and informal leaders in the company, the most influential and symbolic people. It may even include people who have left the company, due to retirement, or individuals who have been there since the company started. These people's role is to *parent* the brand, to take it through the process of development. They can also have a role as a resource team in really important branding issues, as in the context of acquisitions or similar situations, when the brand is at stake or crucial for the identity and further success of the company.

At a practical level, most CEOs need help and support, someone who reports directly and interacts with them, to co-ordinate all branding activities, inside and outside the company, prepare and follow up on strategic decisions regarding the brand, and monitor the usage of the brand. This is how BMW organizes itself. A special team handling branding issues reports directly to the CEO, rather than the marketing director as used to be the case.

Chief Branding Officer

CLEARLY, THE INVOLVEMENT and belief of the CEO are vital. Once the Brand Code has been identified, the CEO has to lead the way by living the brand. Sometimes, CEOs find this difficult. They are worried and not a little daunted by people's expectations. A typical comment is 'I'm not the charismatic leader needed to make this organization truly brand driven.' Such concerns are natural. We can't all be Richard Branson or Jack Welch. There are many different styles of leadership. The most important leadership attribute is to believe in the brand. If you, as the leader, are not prepared to live the brand, then you should resign.

The branding process starts with you. Ask yourself:

How compelling are the organization's goals?

How compelling are your own personal goals?

Many companies have spent a great deal of time on setting goals and there are many different objective-setting schemes. One of the most popular is SMART: Specific, Measurable, Achievable, Realistic, and Time-bound. The end result can be measured in terms of quantity, quality, time, cost, and behaviour. This is all very well, but does it really create motivation and inspiration? Does it really create passion within you, and within your organization? Probably not.

The simple truth is that what makes you tick will most probably make the people around you tick. NLP teaches us to model ourselves and our business on people and businesses that we perceive to be successful. When we do this, we realize that successful leaders and their organizations are not driven by ritualistic goals – although they may have measurable goals to monitor success. They are driven by the compelling vision that comes out of a well-defined and expressive Brand Code.

So how do we start the visionary, uplifting, and motivational process driven by the brand? First you have to reprogramme the people involved – and you have to start with yourself.

Athletes appreciate this. They know that if they think negatively, the result will be negative. If you start worrying about hitting the ball when you're playing tennis, then you will end up missing it. How often do you say to yourself in those situations 'I mustn't do that,' only to find that you keep on doing 'that' over and over again. Successful sports people understand that they become successful by imagining what they would like to be able to do.

The trouble is, if you think about what you should do, or even worse what you must do, you automatically begin to think in terms of what other people – your top management, your board, your friends, or your partner – would like you to do. This won't get you very far.

To get your company onto a new track, to make a successful brand, requires that you do what you and the team re-programming the brand would really like to do. It has to be personally motivating. You need to want avidly to create a successful brand. Successful brand building is done by passion, not by obligation.

The next step is to create what I call a mental movie (a mental picture is not enough, it has to be 'live'), the more vivid the better. The mental movie should be about how it would be to have already done what you want to achieve. Close your eyes and try to imagine how it would feel to have built a highly successful brand.

NLP teaches us to do it like this:

What does it look like?	What are you saying to yourself?
What do you see?	What are others saying?
What is around you?	What sounds are there?
Is there anybody else in the movie?	What does it feel like?
Look around, see all the details	What kind of feelings do you get physically?
What does it sound like?	What touches you?
What do you hear?	What emotions do you feel?

For example, imagine you are going on stage to receive an award for being the best brand in your business, in your country, or even in the world. See the headlines in the articles about your company in *Business Week*, or in some of your national business magazines. Feel the handshake from one of your senior board members thanking you for a good job. Feel the appreciation from people sitting next to you at a dinner, feel their curiosity, feel their interest, hear their questions. Imagine them asking 'how did you do it?' – then imagine your suitably modest but authoritative explanation.

To many people brought up in Lutheran or other truth-demanding cultures, enjoying your success like this *before* it has happened is morally reprehensible. Success is a distant reward, a complete surprise, rather than something fondly and lavishly imagined.

The truth is that if you don't clearly imagine yourself as successful in the future, you will probably not be successful in the future. Programming yourself, creating a positive mental movie, enables you to transfer your enthusiasm to your organization. When the implementation of a Brand Code in an organization fails, it is almost always because managers have failed to transfer their conviction and belief to the people working in the company.

The third step is to act as if your mental movie, based on the Brand Code and its vision, is true. Your unconscious mind does not differentiate between what is imagined and what is real. And anyway, perceived reality is the only reality in the world of branding. The more vividly you see yourself achieving what you want to achieve, the more your unconscious mind will believe that you actually will achieve it, and it will programme you to act as if you will. The more you act as if you have achieved what you want with your brand, the more likely you are to get it exactly as you want it to be. This is human nature.

Once you have established the outcome with all your senses, it begins to gain its own momentum. Stepping into your outcome like this is pure NLP. The power comes from being able to imagine yourself in the future you want. The planning to get there might feel important to you, but believe me, if you strongly imagine yourself as a part of your future, then the steps to get there will lay themselves out automatically in a very natural way. If you live 'inside' your Brand Code, the opportunities to implement it will magically emerge.

There are a few more things to attend to in order ensure success. First, it's very important that you put your outcome in context; put all the circumstances, all the key people involved into your mental movie. When you do this you realize that there might be circumstances for which you would prefer not to be responsible. You may, for example, come to think that the outcome of your branding process depends on other people or on something you feel you can't control. This can be painful, but it dramatically increases the chances of success if you can eliminate these conditions. If you can be in total control of the situation and take on that responsibility it increases your power tremendously.

Sometimes this can be very difficult. But there is a trick for turning your chosen branding outcome into something that is self-maintained and not dependent on other factors – and that is to assign it a higher purpose. Richard Bandler calls this 'chunking up.' The question you should ask is 'What's so important about achieving the outcome of this branding process?' The answer may be better business for your company, higher profits, a better market position, higher financial value, or perhaps something more spiritual.

At a higher level, possible ways open up by which you can achieve your outcome. You may have to do this in several steps; more customers, leading to higher profits, leading to more profit sharing for you, leading to more security for you and your family. The higher you move, the more you focus on yourself and the increasing feeling of the process being under your control.

Another factor to attend to is the calculation of what it will take to achieve the desired branding outcome. What are the risks? What are the feelings or discomfort? Do you have to give up something that you have now? Is there any pain or sadness involved? Is the outcome of the branding worth what it will take? If you decide that the outcome is worth it, then you have the necessary commitment to proceed. If not, you have to think about modifying your desired outcome and, most probably, deciding to do something else instead.

An important checkpoint related to this is to ask yourself what the present situation does for you. Why would you want to maintain the status quo? Maybe it satisfies an important need for you. How does the present state serve you? This might feel strange or perverse, since you want to change that state. Someone who wants to be healthy may find that being unhealthy actually brings more sympathy and attention. Similarly, experience shows that even if a new name for a merged company is the best choice, a new corporate name will cause a temporary feeling of insecurity in people, employees, and customers. It is important to go through these things in your mind so that you know how to deal with them in the future, and how you might work around them in order to achieve your desired branding outcome.

You need also to ask yourself whether the outcome that you want fits with the person you are or the one you want to be. If it doesn't fit, find another outcome to fulfil. It's important that you are in accord with your branding outcome. You will have to be able to step completely into the brand you are creating.

Creating a recipe

WHEN YOU ARE TOTALLY committed to your branding outcome, it is time to take action. But before doing so, one last thing needs to be established. This used to be called the 'business idea.' In the brand-driven company we call it the brand recipe, since it is the recipe for being the superior brand in your marketplace. 'The one with the best recipe will win,' says Paul Romer of the Stanford Research Institute. This recipe is derived directly from your brand code. But when you create it, you should be wary of involving too many chefs. Leave it to the core team charged with re-programming your brand.

The best tool for developing the recipe is something I call the Brand Activity Generator. Simply consider your Brand Code and then ask: what are the ingredients and the combination, or recombination of ingredients, that will provide you with an unbeatable recipe?

Think in 4-D. The functional dimension asks you to think about the unique features that you would be able to give to your product or your company. They could be physical but also beneficial, if it is a service you are offering. Think packaging; the way you label and offer and combine things is as important as the content, technology, or quality of the product or service itself. Be sure to get your bearings from the Brand Code in the center. If the Brand Code, as in the case of Scandinavian Airlines, says 'Simplicity,' then the functional part of the recipe should be to offer simplicity. Think about how to do that.

Now, move to the social dimension. How are you able to create a cult around your company, product, or service? You are looking for something that will be perceived as different and appealing about your brand. For example, Internet company Dobedo offers a unique chat site that encourages the formation of 'clans'; American car manufacturer Saturn offers home-coming parties for its cars.

Next is the mental dimension. How can you create a personal, individual experience in your brand? BMW did it with 'freude am fahren' (the joy of driving) as its main marketing theme, combined of course with the functional ingredient of new technologies such as the car's linked back axis.

Finally, it is worth looking at the possibility of adding a new ingredient or redoing an old one to become the spiritual dimension of your recipe. For an investment fund corporation like KPA in Sweden, its strict ethical investment policy is a strong differentiator. In today's transparent world with no place to hide anything that can be regarded as unethical, it is a good idea to include this dimension when creating your recipe for success.

If you anticipate resistance in the future, it is well worth investing in this dimension in advance.

The most important issue when creating a brand recipe is to add value for the customer, and to make it different and hard for competitors to copy.

Develop rapport

RAPPORT IS THE ABILITY to relate to others in a way that creates trust and understanding. Rapport is the ability to see another person's point of view, without necessarily agreeing with it. Most business decisions are based on rapport rather than product or service superiority. You are more likely to buy from someone you can relate to than someone you can't.

Here, we are interested in building and maintaining rapport between management and staff. Rapport is a necessity if you are to be able to influence. It is the most important prerequisite for successful branding, as it is for communication and development in any organization generally.

There are basically two types of rapport: the one you can actually see with your own eyes, and the one that is deeper, based on beliefs and values. Maybe you have noticed how in some companies (they are usually the most successful) people physically act very similarly. They may move in the same way, use the same posture and gestures, their voices and tones are similar, they use the same words and phrases. They also share beliefs and, quite often, deeper values. IBM is a huge company that created a uniform business style almost akin to the FBI. This psychological phenomenon, the ability and urge to take on the same style, is called 'matching' in NLP jargon.

Sometimes for an outsider this can appear rather ridiculous. But a successful brand creates rapport, and 'the way we are' is usually part of the brand recipe. Corporate symbols and rituals are as effective for the brand as they are for religions.

Some people are very good at establishing rapport, putting people at their ease and thereby opening up communication. With most of them it is a talent, but everyone can learn the ability to create rapport. Excellent communicators are very good at building rapport by paying attention to and matching all existing elements in the natural rapport they observe among people in a company; this is the basis of many consulting businesses.

They are also very conscious of matching as many as possible of the following:

Posture position of the body, legs, feet, weight distribution, positioning of the arms, fingers, shoulder, inclination of the head
Expressions direction of the look, movement of the gaze
Breathing rate and way of breathing
Movement the signature rhythm of people, matching its pace
Voice and language patterns pace, volume, pitch, tone, type of words, intonation.

To access a deep level of rapport a good communicator is able to match beliefs and values. One way to train yourself in matching is when you are an outsider, an observer, and do not have to engage in a conversation. Don't be surprised, if you do it well, if one of the parties you observe turns to you trustingly and asks for your advice.

'Pacing' is another technique used by skilled communicators. It is respect for the state, style, or feelings of others. If someone is concerned, pacing is showing understanding for that concern. If someone is joking, pacing is having fun together with that person.

When you are good at matching and pacing, you are able to lead. 'Match, pace, and lead' are like the principles of eastern martial arts; you go with the force of your fighting partners to take them where you want them to go.

When introducing a new branding idea in a company, you have to do it in exactly the same way. You have to match and pace the existing culture, use its energies (never go against it, but with it), and lead people into the new ideas and the changes that will have to take place.

Important as it is for you personally that the new branding outcome fits your personality, it is also important that it fits the existing culture of your organization. Starting a new company is much easier. But you still have to create a good fit with the personalities of the first employees to form the new company. The easiest way is to invite them to be members of the team re-programming the brand, so they automatically form the cultural core of the company.

Metaphors: visualizing and storytelling

THE MOST IMPORTANT method when implementing your new Brand Code is to use metaphors. A metaphor is a shortcut to the unconscious mind. Metaphors are quite often visual, although auditory and feeling metaphors also exist.

Some of the great breakthroughs in our civilization have come about because of metaphors. Einstein is said to have used metaphors while developing his theory of relativity. As he lay daydreaming he imagined himself riding a sunbeam, and traveling down in an elevator he claimed to have jumped to help him picture how the keys in his pockets moved relative to his trousers and himself.

Metaphors are very common in our language, we say: 'life is a bed of roses,' or 'business has died down,' or 'we can overcome the objections,' or 'we are right on track to achieve what we want.' Metaphors might be single words, sentences, expressions, or stories. Through constructing and telling stories, metaphors enable us to master change and to influence people in a new direction.

The founders of NLP, Richard Bandler and John Grinder, used Milton Erickson to model on. Erickson was a wheelchair-bound hypnotist and therapist and a master of personal change, as well as being a master of metaphors. Among the stories he used was this:

> One day an unknown horse strayed into the yard of the farm where I lived as a child. No one knew where this horse had come from as it had no markings by which it could have been identified. There was no question of keeping the horse – it must have belonged to someone.
>
> My father decided to lead it home. He mounted the horse and led it to the road and simply trusted the instincts of the horse to lead itself towards its home. He only intervened when the horse turned off the road to eat grass or to walk into a field. On these occasions my father would firmly guide it back to the road. In this way the horse was soon returned to its owner. The owner was very surprised to see his horse once more and asked my father, 'How did you know the horse came from here and belonged to us?'
>
> My father replied, 'I didn't know, the horse knew! All I did was to keep him on the road.'

This story tells you a lot about your job of implementing a Brand Code. You are the one guiding your people to stay on the road. This is what branding is all about – staying on the road when there is a lot of grass at the roadside and attractive meadows beckon. You should never deviate from your chosen path to success.

Inside the organization there will be many people, not least your own management colleagues, who interpret the Brand Code in the wrong way. You will then gently have to lead them on to the road again. It is important that you do it firmly but gently, since you do want them to keep their energies, initiatives, and creativity, because you really need all your staff's energy to create a successful brand.

First, it is important to choose the wording of the Brand Code so that it lends itself to a metaphor. When I helped the international network organization of independent auditors and financial consultants BDO, I suggested that we used the initials in their corporate name BDO (originally representing some long-forgotten founders) to explain what their business and brand stood for. The result was BUSINESS, DECISION, ORGANIZERS. How many companies can describe their business idea in three words?

The second aspect of using metaphors when implementing a new Brand Code is to be aware of the metaphors already existing in your company. Does your company describe the workforce as 'troops,' a meeting with angry customers as 'being in the firing line,' or 'attacking the problem,' or 'digging trenches,' or 'aiming at your target'? If so, it may be difficult to change your metaphors overnight to 'a rosy garden' with 'blooming' talents. A gradual change in language is more realistic and preferable.

The metaphors you use are among the most important things to change. The way your people talk is actually the voice of your brand.

The third way of using metaphors in branding is to explain and give emotional depth to your new Brand Code. If you are not already mastering this, you will have to learn how to construct a good story metaphor, or several, explaining different aspects of the Brand Code.

Ingvar Kamprad, the founder of IKEA, came from a very poor part of Sweden, a region called Småland. The people in this region are reputed to be very stingy, saving and re-using everything they can. Instead of using wood to build fences for their cattle, the people of Småland used stone extracted from their fields. These simple stone walls were used by Kamprad visually to tell the story about how he saw the Brand Code, the soul and moral heart of his company.

Some of the best managers in the world use storytelling to convey important messages. General Electric CEO Jack Welch, for example, is a skilled speaker whose autobiographical stories add to his appeal as an inspirational leader. When he talks to GE employees, Welch refers to the giant corporation GE as the 'grocery store,' communicating his brand vision of personal service and the simplicity of a small firm, even though GE is a corporate giant. He also peppers his presentations with personal stories. One story about his childhood illustrates how he learned persistence from his mother, and eventually overcame his stutter. As Welch tells it, he and his mother would drive to the station to pick up his father who worked on the railways. While they waited, they would sit and talk in the dark. His mother refused to acknowledge his stutter, teaching him to go about his business as if he didn't have one.

Similar examples abound from other business leaders, including David Packard, co-founder of Hewlett-Packard, and Ray Kroc of McDonald's fame. What they all have in common is the ability to put a human face on business. Many talented entrepreneurs like this use their own experience, their childhood and early adult life, as a story background to make their points and explain their brands. This is a very good device and one you, too, can use. Go back in your own experience and find a story that can emotionally explain what your brand stands for (and what you as the guardian of the brand stand for). Your metaphor doesn't have to be totally clear or logical. In fact, the best metaphor is one that gives room for the unconscious mind to travel so that it comes to a conclusion of its own. That is why it is useful to leave the metaphor open for explanation in other people's minds. You don't have to provide total clarity. The unconscious mind loves this challenge – it is a common technique used in advertising to strengthen the power and the emotional depth of communication.

Another recommendation for creating metaphors is to make them distant from your everyday reality and business. Too much reality can confuse the recipient and create resistance. But it helps to choose a theme that has a place in the minds of the people you are addressing. For every element in real life you should choose a parallel element in the metaphor. Introduce an element of surprise or a twist at the end of the metaphor – this will excite your listeners and open up their creativity.

Use abstract or general language, which allows listeners' minds to find their own meaning for the words. Use enriched language that appeals to all senses. Act the story out. Improvize when you are telling your story, incorporating in-jokes that you share with your people.

And again, leave it to the minds of your audience to figure out what you really mean by the story. A very important effect when you build a story like this around your new Brand Code is that it actually puts your audience into a kind of trance, and you will have their full, deep attention to an extent that you have not had before. That's why you will never regret the time you spend in preparing your story and developing the skill of telling it. Practice in front of someone you trust and take comments on how you are doing, but most of all tell yourself that you not only *can* do it, but that you also will *love* to do it.

Reframing the organization

CREATING A NEW Brand Code is really all about changing the organization. And changing an organization is as difficult as changing a person. The challenge is that organizations contain many people, not just a single individual.

NLP-based psychology uses an interesting term for this, reframing. A successful branding outcome has a great deal to do with being able to match, pace, and then lead the organization in a new direction. It is easy to get stuck with the old culture, if you match and pace it too well and for too long. Today's managers are often in a hurry to make the change. After all, competitors and customers don't wait for you to change your business gradually, smoothly, and in a psychologically sympathetic way. The result is panic.

Is there a way to still use the momentum of your organization, its present culture, beliefs and values, and channel that energy in a new direction without losing it?

At this point the true value of the Brand Code is clear. The Brand Code can be used to reframe your company. The reason it is so efficient is that the brand represents and reflects the market view, the commercial view, the customer view. It is hard to argue against the Brand Code, and thus it is easily sanctioned by the organization as a driver of change.

The concept of reframing is perhaps best explained by another horse metaphor:

> A father and his son had a farm. They didn't have many animals but they owned a horse. One day the horse ran away.
>
> 'How terrible, what bad luck,' said their neighbours.
>
> 'Good luck, bad luck, who knows?' said the farmer.
>
> Many weeks later the horse returned, bringing with him four wild mares.
>
> 'What marvellous luck,' said the neighbours.
>
> 'Good luck, bad luck, who knows?' said the farmer.
>
> The son began to learn to ride the wild horses, but one day he was thrown off and broke his leg.
>
> 'What bad luck,' the neighbours said.
>
> 'Good luck, bad luck, who knows?' replied the farmer.
>
> A week later the army came to the village to draft all young men to the war. The farmer's son was spared since his leg was broken. Good luck, bad luck, who knows?

Depending on how they are framed, things can be either bad or good. Yesterday's advantage is today's disadvantage and, perhaps, tomorrow's advantage. Just a few years ago people predicted that the Internet would eliminate the need for any middlemen or brokers. Of course, the reality is that there is now a great future for the brokerage of information, and such things as portals and auction sites exist.

To be able to reframe or re-evaluate your business in a new perspective, you need to distance yourself emotionally from it. You need to step aside and use the Brand Code to move the frame so you can see what there is in the culture and competence of the company that can be used in a new way, maybe sometimes combined in a new way or presented differently.

A well-established chain of print shops specializing in copying blueprints for architects has a vanishing market, but can now see the possibility of reframing itself to be a new type of print-on-demand bookshop for the growing web-publishing market. In this process, the organization has to be aware of the new demands that this will make on it, everything from locations and service attitudes to pricing. The new Brand Code creates a new frame.

The Brand Code™ tour

WHEN YOU HAVE a Brand Code, a strong personal motivation, a recipe, and a metaphor, you are equipped to start what I call the Brand Code Tour. Imagine yourself as a rock star taking a great new show on tour to meet your audience face to face.

A new Brand Code is *not* something you introduce via an intranet or e-mail. There is no substitute for people-to-people communication. It is best to meet people in their own environment; it gives them security and cultural continuity. It also shows that you respect them, you come to them and not vice versa. Furthermore, it gives you an opportunity to see life from their perspective. But the real reason for coming to visit them, especially if you are in top management, is that what you have to say to them is clearly so important that you don't hesitate to come yourself.

Before starting your presentation, it is good to comment on and reflect over things that you experience, positive and negative things that you promise to work for to change. Such a promise supports the idea of change that you will then introduce.

It is good to do the Brand Code presentations in smaller groups rather than larger ones. Your agenda is very simple.

Present your new Brand Code, if you prefer against the background of a future scenario. If you like you can use a moodboard, an illustration you and your team have selected to describe the future as you see it and where the brand is designed to fit, then the recipe, and finally sum up with a metaphor that gives the presentation depth. While feedback and dialogue are essential on every other occasion it is important that you don't allow the opinions of your audience to destroy the energy that you have now built up.

Then give them an opportunity to be *creative*, to use the Brand Code, to presuppose it by putting it into their everyday life. First, brief them on the Brand Mind Space that your brand team has created. Then divide them in groups of three to five to work through the four dimensions of branding. This can involve a range of activities. Salespeople may think about how

Brand Activity Generator

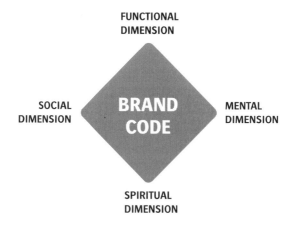

the Brand Code can be transferred to the 'functional' details of their sales work, for example how to change their presentations. Receptionists might consider how to build the Brand Code 'socially' with visitors. Human resource people might see an opportunity of using the Brand Code as a new 'mental dimension' in career planning and workforce development. The research director sees a challenge in using the Brand Code for development in the 'spiritual dimension,' creating a more ethical product. And so on.

For an IT company, some of the elements that emerged were:

Functional Dimension Packaging, Methods, Practice, Presentations, Special Competence, and so on.

Social Dimension Entertainment, Events, Networking, Customer References, Creating a Community, and so on.

Mental Dimension Customer Education, Mentoring, Seminars, Books, Messages, and so on.

Spiritual Dimension Sponsorship, Events, Programmes, Seminars, Mentoring, Books, Websites, and so on.

Note that the most important thing is not what comes out of this exercise, it is actually the making of it. Instead of pointing the energies of your staff into evaluating the Brand Code, criticizing it, or even speculating about what it might mean to them in a negative way, you put them in a positive, creative mood. Instead of breaking down and analyzing, you ask them directly to use the Brand Code to build the future.

Remember that they are all actors on the stage willing to play – now you have assigned them a role to play. What you do is begin to ask them to interpret the role of the Brand Code personally.

It is important to give your audience feedback on what they have come up with. Go through the outcome together, comment, and develop as you comment, be positive, and give them credit.

What has taken place is a magical thing; your Brand Code has automatically been transferred from you to them through this first creative session. Set up a system to keep this process alive. As long as your staff feel that they are allowed to create things based on the Brand Code, judged by the Brand Code, your company gets the power from within to develop, and the guidance of the Brand Code to avoid deviation and lack of clarity.

Always yours

TO HAVE THE Brand Code handy and always there, I recommend that you produce a constant reminder in the form of a very simple little folder, credit-card size, containing the Brand Code, with explanations and the Brand Mind Space of your brand. It should be given to every employee, and serves as a short, practical presentation of what the company they work for stands for. This can also be put on the Web, and from there be transferred as an icon to your computer desktop.

The point of having it on your computer or in your wallet is simply that you always carry the Brand Code with you, and even if you soon learn it by heart, it's good to use with other people in discussion. You should, of course, yourself be the real ambassador by using the reminder on every available occasion.

The brand moves on. It is important to let people inside the organization interpret the Brand Code. And, in order to leverage the brand-building potential, a great deal of freedom and creativity is necessary – although still inside the framework of the Brand Code. Clearly, the creativity has to stop short of changing the Brand Code. If you allow your organization this amount of freedom, you must have a way to monitor, follow up, and control all the activities taking place to build the brand. You have to be able to see that everything is working in the right direction.

There is always a risk in any organization that branding activities are used as a vehicle for career enhancement, or as part of personal development. We all have a tendency to give priority to activities that will give short-term personal benefits rather than long-term branding effects for the whole organization. It is therefore very important to have a controlling – or you might say guiding – function within brand management.

Most of this work can obviously be done within the organization, but in some cases it is useful to have an independent external opinion. For example, managers high up in the organization might be a problem. I used to work for an organization that had a very distinct branding idea that was not in line with, for example, sponsoring of high-end sports like golf or sailing. The problem was, however, that the CEO was crazy about golf. He had sponsored his favourite golf course for many years and he encouraged his co-workers to take up the game. No one in that organization dared to contradict him. In situations like this – and they are common – it is vital to have an independent external controller who is able to point out misleading activities.

The independent controller should be really independent, in other words not with your advertising agency or PR firm. You should chose someone, a management or branding consultant, who is loyal to the Brand Code but without direct interest in implementing it.

Finally, to manage all the organization's different branding activities, it is important to gather them together properly. A tool we use with our clients is an intranet website we call the Brand Monitor. The idea is to be able to monitor every activity that might affect the perception of the brand. Everyone that is working with branding activities in some way should be connected to this website.

Actually, it is more appropriate to call the Brand Monitor an ongoing process. It is mandatory for everybody who is part of the process internally and externally, including the advertising agency, PR company, Web designer and so on, to supply their material to the site. If they don't do this, they might get a warning, and if they still don't participate, we will withdraw the access code to the site, and recommend that the client terminate the contract with that supplier.

The website itself does not have to be very complicated. What is important is to gather the information so the brand management, including the independent controller if you have one, can drive the development of the brand and control it.

6

"Reputation is the real estate of the new economy. Many start-ups spend the bulk of the money they raise just trying to establish a brand."

Invitation to 'First Tuesday', in April in London 2000

MANAGING THE 4-D BRAND

Measuring brands the 4-D way

ALL THIS TALK ABOUT metaphors, stories and NLP runs counter to historical business wisdom. Generation after generation of business leaders have been trained to calculate their way to success. They have rationalized, analyzed, and number crunched. They have strategized and formalized. They have managed according to facts and formulae.

In reality, what characterizes the most successful business people is their intuition about others, their pragmatic, and often almost philosophical, way of treating people. It took me a while to realize this, because as a communicator you tend give your fullest attention to those you communicate with, rather than the people who manage the company you work for. People matter. Great managers and great leaders make people the cornerstone of their organizations and of their jobs.

The analytical and personal remain poles apart. Look at the array of recent mega-mergers and acquisitions (M&As). Calculations of synergies are an important driving force in M&As. It doesn't appear to matter if these calculations are based on little more than guesses and estimations. Analysts should know by now that 2 + 2 rarely equals 5. The truth is that nobody really knows what will happen in a particular merger. Each case is more or less unique.

As more than half of the value of a company can often be related to the brand, one would assume that the brand and its value would be researched in detail. Brand valuation would appear integral to virtually all M&As. In reality, it seldom happens. In many cases the brand is not financially evaluated at all. Its financial value is simply estimated, and negotiated accordingly. Not surprisingly, a properly executed financial evaluation of a brand almost always shows a different value than expected – with the brand usually being worth more.

Opinions vary on every deal. I have heard comments from quite a few brand consultants and about the SEK50 billion ($6 billion) paid for Volvo when the car brand was bought by Ford. Some suggest that the right price should probably have been at least SEK75 billion ($9 billion). Evaluation is difficult without every single detail.

To avoid selling your business too cheaply, the general lesson is to pay more attention to the value of the brand, and what it actually does for your business and could do, or not do, for somebody else if acquired. To do this you have to shift your view or 'paradigm.'

You have to begin thinking not so much in terms of calculated practical, technical, or economic synergies, but more in psychological terms. For example, what does a takeover of a successful competitor mean in terms of motivation among the people in the competitor's organization, and what effects on morale would a takeover have in your own organization?

When Volvo trucks tried to acquire Scania trucks – both Swedish companies and international market leaders – there was a real risk that Scania workers might lose the motivation to attend to every little detail in making their trucks in their normal focused way. Their perception was that the difference in detail was what constituted the difference between the two brands. This personal feeling of 'sameness,' deflating the differentiation value, would most probably spread to influential customers, and in the end make it difficult for Scania, the 'Rolls-Royce' of trucks, to maintain a price premium on its brand. In a calculation, or in the eyes of a financial analyst, the acquisition would look very good, promising some logical synergies in a competitive market. But as the calculation is built on present premium pricing of the Scania brand, losing this would probably change the whole basis for calculating synergies. The psychology of the brand is routinely neglected in situations like this. (Luckily, in this case the merger never happened. The EU Commission vetoed it and, instead, Scania was partially taken over by Volkswagen (the VAG group) From a branding perspective this made more sense as VW didn't have any competing businesses.).

Traditional methods of measuring brands do so in terms of awareness, attitude, and knowledge. Awareness measuring covers how well known a brand is; attitude measuring seeks to evaluate whether the brand generally has a positive or negative perception in the market; and knowledge measuring assesses whether the audience can connect the brand to the correct products or business, or what they know about the brand. This traditional brand research is very general, and even if it is broken down into more detailed information, you seldom really know what to do with it, or how to relate it to something. There might have been some more profound attempts to improve brand research, but I have found this whole field is rather conservative and unimaginative.

Ideally, brand research and measurement should be integrated with the development of the brand. Too often, a great deal of expensive research is put to no use at all when developing the brand. The ideal research instrument must be the same as that used to create your brand, its product development, activities, communication, and design. There needs to be total transparency between research into the market and the competition be-forehand, targeting, generating ideas to develop the brand, and then at the end of the cycle to be able to measure your result in the minds of the people in the audience.

Customer Research Instrument

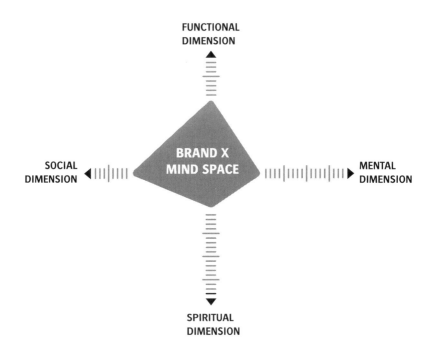

In partnership with a research company, I have developed a unique research technique surveying the Mind Space of the individual being interviewed. This is based on questions and statements covering the four dimensions. The research is conducted in individual interviews on the telephone, on-line via the Web, or by postal questionnaire, and the results can be statis-tically interpreted to include a regression analysis. The result shows not only what the ideal Brand Mind Space of a brand in a category should be, but also how the Brand Mind Spaces of brand A, B, C, etc. in the market compare. And it also indicates how the brand loyalty for each brand is driven by certain dimensions. This research also provides the traditional measurement of the awareness, attitude, and knowledge factors.

Customer research based on the Brand Mind Space can be very valuable for determining the strength and, indirectly, the value of the brand.

> **There are basically three different methods of financially evaluating a brand:**
>
> **COST-BASED VALUE,** in which you either try to estimate the accumulated costs for building the brand in today's monetary value, or calculate the alternative costs, as if you were going to build an equal brand again from scratch.
>
> **REVENUE-BASED VALUE,** which is simply the current value of the expected future earnings of the brand.
>
> **TRANSACTION-BASED VALUE,** in which the market prices of a similar brand acquired recently, or the licensing fees of a brand in the same category, are compared.

Revenue-based evaluation is the most common, because the other methods are difficult to do. But in calculating the future earnings of the brand there is always a problem with setting an appropriate discount rate. It is the strength of the brand that decides the rate, and the best way to determine the strength is to measure the loyalty – the brand's ability to produce satisfied customers who would purchase the brand again, or recommend it to others.

As I mentioned earlier, the regression analysis in a customer research programme based on measuring the Brand Mind Space makes it possible to calculate the factors driving loyalty. A high correlation between customer expectations and the four dimensions as well as the measured Brand Mind Space of the brand to be evaluated indicates high customer loyalty. A high number of loyal customers results in a price and volume premium and a lower discount rate. Finally, the brand market value can be calculated based on that loyalty.

It won't be long before companies conduct an annual brand audit in the same was every company now audits its accounts on an annual basis. Because the brand is often the single most important asset in a company, and the most important factor in generating revenues, its evaluation will inevitably become part of the official Annual Report of most companies. Already environmental and intellectual capital audits are beginning to complement the traditional financial report.

But you shouldn't wait for an annual brand audit to become mandatory. The farsighted brand manager will start now with an annual (or more frequent) audit of the strength of the brand, following up the activities that have been implemented. This process can be done very extensively or less thoroughly, but what is important is to make the brand audit a natural process in the organization. This helps with the ongoing nature of branding.

An Annual Brand Audit basically starts with measuring the brand. The question is, how well is the expected Brand Mind Space fulfiled? The next step is to review the activities for implementation and suggest a change in planning for the following year. An adjustment in the Brand Code might also be appropriate, although this should be done with great sensitivity.

A financial audit of the brand value can be included in the audit. This is very valuable to get a static monetary value of the brand to match with the costs of the brand-building process. When the monetary value of the brand is presented, it engenders respect internally for the importance of all activities that maintain or develop the brand.

The brand and the organization

ONE BRAND, ONE COMPANY, and one message has always been a marketing person's dream. In practice, the dream has proved elusive. Why is this the case? In part it is human nature. Reputations are not built by doing more of the same, but by inventing new messages and entirely new brands. In every part of a big organization there will be people who have the ambition, the creativity, and the drive to build a new brand. These people are natural entrepreneurs who happen to find themselves working for a corporation. Every organization needs these people to be dynamic. But at the same time they can cause problems, not least if you aspire to a consistent, well-defined brand and an equally consistent brand message.

It is already clear that in the next few years there will be huge changes in organizational patterns. From a branding perspective this will not necessarily be for the better. In the flat, networked organization, entrepreneurs will have more space and more scope to be entrepreneurial. The whole idea is to create an environment that allows them to flourish.

The difficult thing will be to find a way to hold the organization together, to bind it into a coherent whole. I believe that the brand will play that role. These new organizational entrepreneurs – some call them intra-preneurs because they operate inside a corporate network – will value the brand because it will give them leverage outside the organization, while keeping them aligned with the internal organization.

In fact, the brand is for the network corporation what the hierarchy was for the old industrial organization. It is its guiding mechanism, and its most important driver. The brand can provide new entrepreneurs with a structure or framework. But it will be hard to keep them from messing around with your corporate brand or your leading product brands. Brand discipline will have to be enforced.

At this point it is very important that *you* know what you are doing with your brand. Let's summarize what we have discussed about this issue so far. These are the most important organizational rules when it comes to branding:

FIRST RULE

Never invite everybody to decide what your brand stands for. The Brand Code should be set up exclusively by a small group of people who should decide what the brand stands for and then communicate it to the organization.

SECOND RULE

Give a lot of space to the people inside your organization to interpret the Brand Code. Encourage creative, entrepreneurial people to be actively involved in that process. Enlist their help to translate and reinterpret the Brand Code continuously through new products, new business ideas, and new messages.

THIRD RULE

Monitor your brand carefully. You just might have to jump in and correct or adjust some of the Brand expressions, or emphasize the Brand Code and give support to certain initiatives.

If you follow these three simple rules you will be able to use your brand, and its Brand Code, to manage both a network organization full of entrepreneurs and a more hierarchical one, with people in different roles who want to make a career out of being creative and taking initiatives.

The brand, motivation and recruitment

THE BRAND CODE IS, by its sheer simplicity, a people-motivating device. The attitude of many companies is that simply drawing a salary every month is all people should require to be motivated. That is no longer true – if it ever was. For those who can get a job, and hold on to it, remaining motivated takes a lot more than that. To be motivated you need to feel good about what you are doing. The first, very important step for any company that wants to motivate its people (and again, that's what the talented entrepreneur is so good at) is to communicate what the company stands for. If that is well matched to what the employee wants out of life, then the person will feel motivated. Sometimes that means that someone will turn down a better-paid job for one that they find more motivating.

The code with its six inputs and its core message answers the questions that most people ask of their employer:

> What is the customer benefit of our product, service and company? (Will what I do make me appreciated among my friends?)
>
> What is this company's positioning, what makes it special? (How can it make me special?)
>
> What is the style of this company? (What am I supposed to be like, and how does that fit with who I am?)
>
> What is the mission, the role in society for this company? (Will it make me feel that I'm doing something worthwhile with my life?)
>
> What is the vision in this company, what kind of future does it have? (What future will I have if I choose to work with these people?)
>
> What are the values of this company? (What values do I stand for, do the company's values match my own?)
>
> And then finally the core message of the Brand Code, how do I feel about working for a company with this kind of message? (Is it fulfilling?)

So to use the Brand Code to motivate people simply has to do with communicating it, and training people not only to think about it, but to use it in a creative way – for everything, every day.

The brand and product development

THERE ARE MANY WAYS to generate new product ideas. One is to imitate what other businesses are doing and put it into your own business context. Another way is to be guided by technology and your own fantasies or wishes. This is the most common approach.

But a third way, which can be very powerful, is to watch consumers. Imagine that you are an anthropologist studying and documenting an unknown culture, and then analyzing it in a multidisciplinary group of people. The aim is to try to invent things, products or services, as solutions that make life easier for the users. The Doblin Group in Chicago specializes in this type of product development. The company often uses video cameras to record hours and hours of customer behaviour, footage that is later analyzed by a group of people from many disciplines – engineers, humanists, behavioural scientists, psychologists, IT specialists, web designers, and communication specialists.

One of my favourite examples is some work that the Doblin Group carried out for an American chain of gas stations. Thousands of hours of video footage were collected documenting how people fill up their cars. On most of these takes the researchers observed the same thing, the person facing the car turned their head around, stretching their neck to watch the amount of gas, or the amount of cash, on the front of the gas pump. The multidisciplinary team watching this decided to move all the information from the pump, making it dumb. Instead, they equipped the handle with a digital display showing not only quantity and the cash amount, but also making it possible to preset the desired amount with the thumb. No more neck-aching bending – all the focus is on the handle. This innovation made these stations really different in a market where service is generic.

The outcome of an approach like this is a catalogue of new ways to look at old issues, and to create something that really can add difference to the brand.

Adding difference is the key. Sony is one of many brands in its market. But through inventions it has been able to create a special position in the electronic gadgets market. The company's inventions – from the Walkman to the PlayStation – have always shown high differentiation. The company has a strong entrepreneurial leadership and a Brand Code demanding mass-market, mind-breaking new technology.

Underpinning this are its stated values. These are:

Elevation of the Japanese national culture and status

Being a pioneer – not following others, but doing the impossible

Respect and encouragement of individual ability and creativity

Microsoft, with its Windows partners, has created a flow of new software applications for all kinds of activities in offices as well as in homes. The driving idea behind this has been Bill Gates's vision, 'A computer on every office desk and in every home,' accompanied by the Microsoft tag line, 'Where do you want to go today?'

There are numerous examples of other companies that have produced more astonishing products – technically superior, and the first of their kind – but without being able to use this inventiveness to build the brand. Usually the reason for this is that the products have not been created with the brand in mind. Instead, they have been created by clever engineers who wanted to impress colleagues and management, and in some cases also wanted to advance their own careers.

Philips is a good example of this. It became a strong household brand largely because of its long history, rather than its inventiveness in creating new products. Almost all of the standards in hi-fi and video technology have their origin in Philips, from compact cassettes, to CDs, to DVD. The voice recognition system, introduced as a new feature on the Ericsson T28 mobile phone, was actually a Philips feature used on its own mobile phones a year or so earlier. But if you compare Philips to Sony, or to Nokia, you will understand what I mean by developing products as part of the Brand Code, rather than for their own sake.

Extending the brand

A GOOD BRAND can be a fantastic vehicle for transferring value – from the owner of the brand to the customer, but also from a branded product in one category to a product in another category. In fact, extending the power of a brand into new products and services is one of the strongest reasons for investing in brand building. The commercial base for the brand investment gets larger – as does the profit. But this transfer of value doesn't come without complications.

It is often difficult to decide if and how to extend a brand. Basically there are two types of extensions. The first is *line extension*, which involves an extension of the brand in the same category of products or services – usually in the form of variations, new tastes or recipes. Absolut Vodka is a good and successful example; Absolut Lemon, Absolut Mandarin, and Absolut Currant, supported by ingenious advertising, succeeded in expanding the brand.

The other type of extension is *brand extension*, which involves using an existing brand in new categories of products or services. For example, the Calvin Klein brand is used not just to sell underwear, but also eyewear and perfume. Virgin is perhaps the greatest exponent of this.

How do you decide what is going to work? First you have to analyze your brand – honestly, and without too much wishful thinking. The basic rule is that the more philosophical content your brand has, and the stronger its position in the market – that is, the more differentiated it is – the better its prospects in another product category. If, on the other hand, it is a product type of brand, with a weaker and less differentiated position in the market, then you might be able to line extend, especially if you can provide support through a very good distribution network, but brand extension is unlikely to succeed.

The Basic Rules of Brand Extension

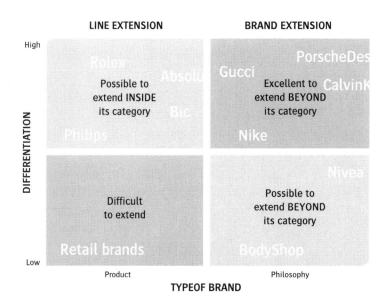

There are many examples of successful brand extension, usually among fashion brands; these tend to be stronger brands with a higher philosophical component and a higher degree of differentiation than other brands. But not all of them have been successful. Some have extended their brand too far without adequate control. Take Pierre Cardin, for example, once a very exclusive designer brand, now totally degenerated because of careless usage, branding products without quality and distinction. Gucci was about to follow the same path but has recovered, partly because it imposed some order among its many licenses. The recovery of Gucci also had to do with the retro phenomenon that has saved so many brands from falling from grace.

A great deal can be learned from some classic mistakes. The BIC brand, for example, established its position in the market as 'the disposable item' brand, starting with the disposable ballpoint pen, then moving to the disposable razor and disposable lighter. When constructing the gas container for the lighter, the engineers at BIC realized that they had invented a disposable container that could be used in many other ways. One of their ideas was to use it for perfume; an inexpensive perfume, distributed in an ingenious container, and sold in the same places where the BIC lighters and pens already were. The concept was a catastrophe. The consumers associated the product with fuel rather than cosmetics. It lacked the glamor and credibility of a fashion brand. The BIC brand is highly differentiated, but tied to certain products and a specific technical knowhow, so it didn't work. If the idea had been tied to a philosophy brand like a fashion brand instead, the technical solution might have supported the brand philosophy and been successful. The step from Marlboro cigarettes to Marlboro lighter to Marlboro aftershave, for example, might have worked better.

What you can learn from this is that ideas generated by your own people might fit better under another brand rather than your existing one. So why not sell it and make some money out of it, instead of undermining the value of your own brand?

The most important point here is that in order to extend your brand and benefit from it in other business areas, your best bet is to build a philosophy brand, to create a brand that stands for something.

What is a philosophy brand? Is Harley-Davidson a philosophy brand, for example? To start with it was definitely a product brand, very much like Rolex. But the values that built Harley-Davidson are illustrative in showing how a product brand can make the transition into a philosophy brand and be successful in brand extensions in the way that Harley-Davidson is, with its clothing products, cafés, and so on. Notice, too, that by these brand extensions Harley-Davidson has managed to stay with its audience – something that Levis has clearly failed to do.

Porsche, with Porsche Design and its brand extensions into eyewear, cameras, household gadgets, and clothing design, is another good example. The car has become a design philosophy.

There is a spectrum when talking about philosophy brands. At one end we have the 'style' brands; at the other end we have the 'deeper' values brands. Generally, the more you move to values on the scale, the more universal your brand becomes in the kind of categories it can adopt. But on the other hand, strong values will place high demands on the products that embrace them.

And the logical next step is precisely that: to establish how much you can extend the philosophy of your brand over product and service categories – or, rather, what can you possibly incorporate under the same brand philosophy umbrella? In order to find that out, you need to go back to your Brand Code and match the new product or service idea to that and see how it works.

In order to use your Brand Code to create new products, services, or business concepts, make line or brand extensions, enter new markets (and as described later also to acquire new business, select partners, and so on), you need a decision tool. The Brand Code can be used to generate ideas, but also to 'frame' your ideas with the help of your brand. The most important thing is the framing. You quite often come across situations in which you have to decide if a product fits your brand or not. If the latter is the case, it might need a brand of its own, or would be better under another existing brand.

I have invented a device for this brand framing called the BrandEnvelope. It is the Brand Activity Generator (see page 142) inside a hexagon with the six Brand Code inputs as the frame.

This is how you use it.

Create the new product or service, line or brand extension, and so on, using the Brand Activity Generator inside the hexagon. Put the Brand Code in the middle and start working on ideas for creating a new product featuring functional, social, mental and spiritual dimensions – as many as possible of the dimensions in every product. Then make Brand Code statements for each of the new products, assigning it product, positioning, style, mission, and vision.

Now match the Brand Code of your company with the 'Brand Codes' of your products. Find out if the product is inside the Brand Envelope or not.

If you are not sure see what happens if you try to change the brand, try to stretch the Brand Code to fit the product. If that works it's OK. If it doesn't work, if you feel you are now destroying the old brand, creating a new one might be an option to consider. Don't push your Brand Code too far.

The Brand Envelope

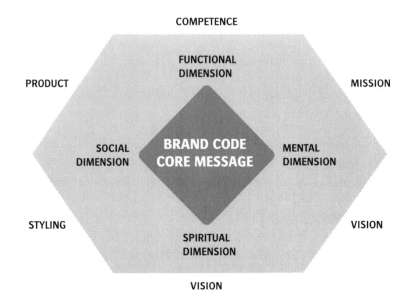

An Austrian health food company asked me if it could devise a healthy pizza and put this under its brand. We had a long discussion about it and using this model I tried to evaluate what kind of Brand Code a pizza like that would have. I did it as fairly as I could. But the obvious problem for any pizza would be its fast food/bad food profile, which was incompatible with the Brand Envelope of this health food brand, even if stretched. Indeed, it could destroy the brand in other product segments. On the other hand, the idea of a healthy pizza was excellent, and my recommendation was to establish a new line of healthy and light fast food under a new brand name.

Naming with a Brand Code™

WHAT'S IN A NAME? A great deal if it is to carry the brand. The bigger the market, the more important it is to have a strong name that is easy to remember. First impressions of your brand will almost certainly be visual, an image, rather than a personal contact and/or experience. In times of change the brand name, and of course the Brand Code on which it is based, is your most important asset. In the end, it is the only thing that remains constant.

> **The name plays a few key roles:**
>
> **Identification** Whatever a customer thinks of a certain brand, he or she will always relate to it in one way or another. By being a part of everyday life of your customers, you build a strong brand.
>
> **Communication** Through the name you send out information about yourself to your surroundings. When the name plays the role of communicator, the message can either be clear, full of nuances, or subconscious.
>
> **A valuable asset** The name can become surprisingly important when the brand is growing. It will be a very special part of your legal property.

A name is not only important, but also complex. It must work in different environments, play different roles and involve many aspects of communication.

When working with a start-up, the name is often the first thing that the client wants my help with. They want me to invent a name, quite often preceded by their own attempt and failure to find and decide on a name. The usual problem is that everybody involved in this naming process has just been 'shooting from the hip.' There is almost never a brand platform from which to start the work; and there is, and this is more important, never a brand platform to base a decision on. As a result, it is hard to say whether one name is better than another, or which name to select, at least to put on to the short list. There is typically urgency to get a name, but no process to achieve it. The reason for this is obvious, without a name you don't really exist.

With naming I recommend doing the brand platform and the Brand Code *first*. Then you can begin the naming process. I have developed my own process for naming, from which I have selected some parts to share with you.

A problem with creating the Brand Code for a company that doesn't exist is that there are usually no managers to do it with. But even if the management and the board members are not yet all in place, you can still do a preliminary Brand Code. Before we talk about the criteria for a good name, let's look at some of the different types of names.

In our daily lives we come across a large number of different trademarks and names. To be honest, you sometimes wonder how on earth they came to this or that name. A name can be clearly descriptive, it can lack meaning, or it can be something in between, quite unclear in its direct message, but one that creates associations.

DESCRIPTIVE NAMES

This category of names describes advantages and attributes in a simple, direct way. The more descriptive, the more directly it communicates with the customer. Less time is needed to explain what the company actually sells. This kind of name has a great advantage – it requires less marketing effort, often activities to create awareness only, and the message can be very simple.

Disadvantages of a descriptive name include the difficulty of crossing language barriers, and the fact that only one out of maybe several advantages can be communicated. Less room is also given to communication with the receiver's subconscious mind. Another disadvantage of choosing this kind of name is the difficulty in legally protecting it, since it is less distinctive. The name CyberCash is not that strong a name, because it is virtually impossible to stop a sound-alike name like CyberMoney or CyberDollars.

Examples of extremely descriptive (and successful) names include Dab-It-Off, Sweet 'n' Low and Yoghurt Juice.

The company originally called Farallon began marketing its services on the Internet in 1998. At the same time it changed its name to Netopia. The change was made at a time when most companies in the Internet business did not use the word net or wired in their names. Netopia communicates a creative utopia on the web, promising something rare and special. It gives the potential customer room for imagination as well as high-technology professionalism. But in recent years there has been a tendency to move away from these kinds of names. The Internet is already moving into its second phase (or maybe third), and the competition between equal concepts is tough. Differentiation has already become an important issue. And the name is a very good device for beginning to differentiate your company or product.

ProcureSoft was the name of a company that developed software to help companies automate their purchase processes by using the Internet. The name described the services of the company quite clearly, but it lacked energy. The management then decided to change the name to Ariba – a more exciting name, promising more.

ASSOCIATIVE NAMES

An associative name does not exactly tell you what the company does, but it clearly indicates the core meaning of the product or service. It also communicates advantages and values, and gives a feeling for the brand. The advantages of an associative name are that it is easily remembered and signals a strong, subconscious message.

However, problems can also arise for associative names. For example, they are sometimes harder to protect because of the lack of distinctiveness. Another problem can appear when the name is used internationally; associations can be different when placed against another cultural background. This can also occur on the domestic market, because all individuals have different associations and everything is perceived reality. I remember a name I produced for an IT company some years ago. This was EGO, a powerful name that of course had some negative associations, but it came out as mostly positive in the younger, western culture. In Malaysia, however, and some other Asian countries that were of interest to the business, we were confronted with a very mysterious negative attitude that was never really explained. The name was dropped – the company is now called iD2, and is a leader in smartcard-based Internet security systems.

Applied Bionomics is another example, a company that helps marine operations to improve their efficiency. The name gave the wrong associations and it was often confused with biotech companies. The company then changed its name to Maxager, indicating management expertise and the ability to maximize the productivity of the workforce.

Visa is an example of a successful name. It does not say anything about finance or about credit cards. Instead, it talks about possibilities, access, opening doors, passing borders, and travel – qualities much more interesting, exciting, and imaginative.

NEOLOGISMS OR COINED NAMES

This category includes names that have no exact meaning. On the contrary, they possess the unique possibility of letting themselves be charged with whatever meaning you prefer. This kind of name often has a special meaning for its founder or owner, it is part of the story of the company, which, as we discussed before, is very important. In these cases the name often serves as a conversation piece, leading into the philosophy and the values of the company. The aspect of the entrepreneur's total freedom plays an important role in this category.

Neologisms are short, strong, and graphically aesthetic names. They are distinctive, original, and ideal for international use because of the minimal risk of linguistic problems. They are also easier to protect legally.

Yahoo! is a very good name, because it does not say anything about the product. It is a name that can be invested with a number of meanings. More often than not, it makes people speculate about what the name really stands for.

When the founder of Kodak, George Eastman, created the name of his company he plucked it out of thin air. It was a short name, powerful and hard to misspell. It did not mean anything, which made it easy to register as a trademark. K was Eastman's favourite letter and he created a name out of this preference. The choice proved to be extremely clever because the sound of K has high distinctiveness and is easily used on the international market.

Another famous name in this category is Pentium. It was created from the idea that this computer chip from Intel was a fifth-generation product. The word 'pente' means five in Greek and the suffix 'ium' was added because it indicated strength.

A negative aspect of a coined name, as mentioned before, is that it usually demands more marketing, because it does not communicate the business you are in or the type of product or service you represent directly to the customer.

**By using the checklist below you can save time and effort
when it comes to choosing a name for your company, product, or service.**

Do not do what others are doing

Go beyond tradition. By leaving the usual categories you create a unique base of communication. Differentiate!

Does it work internationally and in the future?

Is it a good name in, for instance, the Netherlands or Latvia?

What does the Brand Code tell you?

Look especially at the messages about the mission in the Brand Code. What do you want to say to yourself and others? What do you want to do tomorrow? Will the name fit in then? Look at the vision in your Brand Code. Which colour and form are to be found here? Look at styling in your Brand Code. What does this tell you about the name?

Put your world in your name

What is your arena and where do you want to go? Create a universal meaning for the name by using universal morphemes. Again, look at the benefit, competence, style and vision in your Brand Code and in your Brand Mind Space for overall help.

Charge the name with a promise

What promise do you want the customer to feel, think, and experience? The competence, positioning and the mission in the Brand Code will help you.

Tell your story

What makes your company special? What makes you different from the crowd? What added value is generated by using your product or service? Attract customers by telling a unique story. What would happen if you disappeared from the market? Again, positioning, mission, and vision in the Brand Code are helpful. The spiritual dimension of your Brand Mind Space might also get you fired up.

The meaning is not everything

Try to get rid of the pressure to be logical and relevant. Semantics come first, phonetics second. After that the sound. This can be symbolic, since different letters have different sounds that communicate different messages. How does the name feel? What does it sound like? What does it *not* sound like?

Listen to yourself, but don't be too hard on yourself

Don't ask yourself to love the new name. There are no perfect names, no shortcuts to success. The most important thing is that you don't dislike the name yourself. Give every name a chance to be liked. Usually a name becomes more appreciated with time.

In your name you don't need to describe exactly what you do

Product lifecycles are getting shorter, which puts the philosophy of your brand in focus. The name should reflect thoughts, ideas, and philosophy rather than the product and the service you are selling today, as that may be different tomorrow.

Déjà-vu taboo

Words such as pro, global and ultra that are used to form compound names are used too often. Avoid all these boring trends. Names like that don't say anything anyway.

Shades of Orange

'THE FUTURE'S BRIGHT, the future's Orange.' This is not your usual advertising slogan or tag line for a product or service – it is the essence of a brand that shines. By instilling an idea of believing in the future and not fearing it, the Orange brand has managed to persuade consumers that technology can in fact be 'warm and soft,' that large network and service operators can listen to and take care of you. Orange has taken the mobile telecommunications business to another level as one of its strongest brands.

When it was launched in 1994, Orange was going into a market in which operators just sold things and didn't really care about what customers wanted. They put what they had on to the marketplace and expected people to be happy with it. The Orange brand had to challenge a very technical environment, where monopoly-like operators had charging systems that were extremely inflexible for customers. Orange brought choice to the market, based on a long period of building a quality digital network, and developing the right systems, processes, products, and services. The market at the time only had a 5 per cent penetration; now it is over 40 per cent and projected to be at 50 per cent in a year's time.

Orange looked at the branding opportunities and in this process it went back and looked at how it behaved as a company as part of its overall branding strategy. It brought forward the values that best identified what it was: straightforward, honest, refreshing, dynamic, and friendly. This fitted the organization's internal values. It incorporated these values into the brand platform as part of what the brand stands for. Pulling the brand together and making it distinct is also part of exciting the marketplace with the appropriate external communication and gaining the right brand perception among customers.

Orange has been consistent in its approach. It embraced the adage 'treat people the same way you would like to be treated;' in this case, treat your customers according to the same values you adhere to internally. The traditional style of communication in many technical industries has been rather harsh and commercially exploitative – this is where Orange has come in and done the opposite.

The rationale, according to Orange, for having a very warm, approachable, and accessible brand – softer and friendlier than your competitors – is that it works in both business and consumer markets.

Orange's strategy was to build a reputation for the best service, best-performing network, and best value. The company claims that it has been consistent in communicating itself as a single point of contact – as the customer's one-stop shop, a trusted brand as service provider. Naturally, some of the other players in the field have attempted to imitate this. Competitors have tried to adopt the same type of attitude in their brands. They are beginning to realize the benefits of managing end-to-end customer relationships. Vodafone, for example, has acquired a number of brands and applied a very striking red-on-black identity to all of them (not far from the Orange on black). What does this imply? Being in the same sector means less distinction between all the operators and major confusion for customers as the players start to look and behave in the same way, which makes the differentiation aspect less noticeable.

Orange has been clever in always speaking about the future. The company makes sure it stays ahead, in particular by pushing new technologies and converting these into services and products that are beneficial in making customers' lives better. It offers 'current and future solutions,' while other companies have offered merely the 'latest technology.'

In its strategy, which builds on the positive outlook for the future, the company states 'Our philosophy is to make the world a better place.' This is intended to imply that Orange will ensure that the way we communicate will get better as we move into the future; we'll get more out of life rather than less. This could be thought of as the true Orange mission, bringing the brand into the future with confidence and care.

Orange insists that its values always have to be consistently adhered to wherever the brand is used. This is especially important when considering use of the brand in a joint venture or licensing agreement. These businesses have to be oriented to match the Orange brand values. Whether you are in London or Tel Aviv, wherever anyone comes across Orange, the brand behaves in the same way.

The challenge lies in sustaining the brand idea as a mental image in the customer's mind. The battle to stand out and succeed in the marketplace takes place in the mind of the prospect, that is, your potential customer. They will be attracted to the brand if it aspires to be something, taking on a distinctive role that helps it stand out from its competitors. This is especially important in an industry in which the players are plentiful.

Once again, examining the Orange brand in 4-D is illuminating:

FUNCTIONAL DIMENSION

Technology has to be made useful and simple for the customer to understand. Orange does this by looking at what the technology can deliver, and how it can build state-of-the-art technology into products and services that people really want. In this way it anticipates what the technology can do and what benefits customers might want from it. Rather than challenging customers to adapt to the technology as other brands do, Orange reverses this, it almost challenges technology to be 'adapted' to benefit customers in their everyday use. Technology must also be perceived as easy to use and genuinely useful, with no hassle. Orange's approach to technology is 'soft,' presenting it in as friendly and accessible a way as possible to the customer.

Orange Brand Mind Space

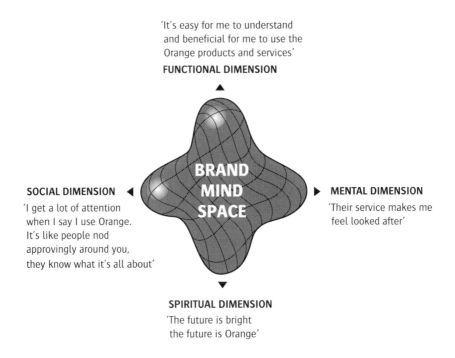

'It's easy for me to understand
and beneficial for me to use the
Orange products and services'

FUNCTIONAL DIMENSION

SOCIAL DIMENSION

'I get a lot of attention
when I say I use Orange.
It's like people nod
approvingly around you,
they know what it's all about'

BRAND MIND SPACE

MENTAL DIMENSION

'Their service makes me
feel looked after'

SPIRITUAL DIMENSION

'The future is bright
the future is Orange'

SOCIAL DIMENSION

Orange has the ability to affect how people see themselves in a positive way as they are using Orange. In relation to others who also use this brand, it is a way of belonging to and feeling you are part of special group of people.

MENTAL DIMENSION

Orange has worked to become associated with the best service in its field. It positions itself as the customer's flexible service hero, rather than a large and inaccessible technical corporation that doesn't care about service. As a customer using Orange you perceive service not just as getting a call through or being billed the right amount. It is more about being looked after; you feel more confident that you get what you signed up for and that makes you feel better.

SPIRITUAL DIMENSION

The overall business idea and brand-building efforts for the Orange brand build on the company's positioning statement and philosophy. It wants to reshape hard-to-understand technology to the benefit of customers in their everyday lives and in the long run for society as a whole. Orange's consistency in building the brand around 'the future's bright, the future's Orange' and the idea of making 'the world a better place' surely improves the possibility of the brand's gaining the right mindset among customers for a long time to come.

Connecting with people

ONE OF THE MOST important reasons for creating this whole methodology for branding was to devise an instrument to stimulate creativity in communication of the brand. Most of the international agencies have devices to formulate the brand message. Most of these are constructed by non-creatives, that is planners or strategists with different backgrounds to the people who have to come up with original ideas. The large consumer goods advertisers, like Procter & Gamble or Nestlé, also have methods for creating briefs that basically contain the same ingredients as my models.

Yet there is a great difference in feeling, attitude, or whatever you like to call it. My aim is to have as few restrictions as possible. Instead, I want to open up possibilities, to initiate associations that can lead to unique solutions in communications and activities supporting the implementation of the Brand Code in the minds of all stakeholders (not just the customer or prospects, of course). Many of the briefing formats I have seen are too prescriptive. They are inhibiting. The people behind the briefing have gone too far, indicating or even recommending solutions. Since these usually are logical deductions from the brief, they become useless for a creative mind; like dirt on the windshield, they clutter up a mind that has to be wide open and clear to receive unconventional ideas.

Sometimes the briefing is too limiting to be of value for a creative person. At the same time, all creative work is about being creative within the frame of a problem, and to have a Brand Code to check one's ideas against is absolutely necessary. Too much of a creative person's time is usually spent on trying to define, to guess what the brand stands for, and that time is much better spent on experimenting with ideas that could provide a solution, instead of first creating a Brand Code.

Every creative person in advertising, product development, or any other activity or discipline concerned with transferring a brand experience should have a right to be supplied with a Brand Code to which they can refer.

I have found it very useful to get some help to spin my creative mind off by using the Brand Activity Generator. This is one of my favourite tools, combining the Brand Mind Space and Brand Code. It is in fact the Brand Code Core Message placed in the middle of the Brand Mind Space.

The idea is to place the Brand Code Core Message there as an initiator and a reference, while your creative mind works with the four dimensions: functional, social, mental, and spiritual. You start by reflecting on the Brand Code Core Message (maybe you think about the whole Brand Code with its six inputs as well). Then you ask yourself, what could you do to transfer that Brand Code to a person's mind using the functional dimension, that is, what should be the nature of activities or communication of a brand with a Brand Code like that? Think about the informative, educational, knowledge-based aspects here, but also about the design and style of the brand. To guide you on style, there is obviously a part of the Brand Future Code stating what kind of style the brand is supposed to represent. For instance, SAS with 'simplicity' in its Brand Code is able to manifest that in its simplified, modern, and very aesthetic design of livery and uniforms.

Then move to the social dimension for the social aspects of the brand. Here we deal with being able to form a community around the brand. Think about get-together activities, in the physical world as well as in the virtual. For example, Nokia has created Club Nokia as an institution for the after-market of its clients. It's there to help you wherever you are with pre-programmed numbers all over the world, a quite natural spin-off of the Nokia Brand Code Core Message 'Connecting People.' In the communication message, you might be able to play on the social feelings or behaviour that the brand originates or causes. This can be especially helpful when thinking about commercials and video.

The Mental dimension might give some idea of a deeper message of trust, security, or self-confidence that can spark ideas for activities or communication messages. For the Swedish Lotto the mental dimensional Brand Code Core Message of 'Keep your dreams alive' has been the advertising theme for more than a decade and led to many award-winning commercials. In one of the commercials, an employee suddenly dares to ridicule his boss by making funny faces in front of him, after a dream of his has been achieved by winning on Lotto.

The Spiritual dimension does not necessarily mean that you should start by donating a great deal of money to some good cause. This is, of course, still a possibility, but you can also do things to help straight away. Take the international network firm of auditing and financial advisers, BDO, which has chosen to support business start-ups with free advice. Or Ben & Jerry's, which named an ice-cream 'Totally Nuts' to satirize the craziness of the members of the US Congress at that time, voting to maintain military spending when the Cold War had already ended. The Spiritual dimension offers a multitude of possibilities to reach beyond the logic of the product of the brand. It concerns public interest and can thus be both a great PR device as well as an efficient differentiator.

Obviously, product development people are the ones who are triggered the most by the Functional dimension. Airlines are good examples of this, not least British Airways and SAS – they are all using the functional dimension for branding.

Customer relations people and those in relationship marketing enjoy the Social dimension, as do sponsoring and event marketing specialists, and community builders on the web.

Examples of this can be found in the automobile industry, such as Saturn and its homecoming parties, when 45,000 car owners return to the factory with their Saturn cars. Or Volkswagen with its sponsoring of the Rolling Stones' tours, and recently the fantastic entertainment center Car City between Wolfsburg and Hanover, starting with Expo 2000.

Of course Lego, with its five tremendously successful Legolands, visited by more than 40 million people each year, has long understood how to sell toys using the Social dimension.

The Mental dimension can be of interest for advertising people looking for an 'inner' message, communication with the consumer on a deeper level. One of the best examples of this is Nike with its 'Just Do It' communication. One of my all-time favourites is the computer company Sperry (which later became Unisys), with its brilliant 'We have learnt to listen' corporate marketing activity conducted over many years, including 'listening training' for all its employees.

The Spiritual dimension is again a favourite among PR people and is used inside the organization by human resource managers, sometimes by the two groups combined. It is interesting how many new brands have used exceptionally generous internal programs for employees to make a difference externally on the Spiritual dimension. Ben & Jerry's ice cream is just one example of a company announcing proudly, publicly on the web its staff development programmes.

Acquisitions with The Brand Code™

TO USE THE Brand Code for acquisitions may sound somewhat strange to some strictly business-oriented people. This is probably correct, as most of the acquisitions over the last ten years have been driven by pure business thinking rather than thinking in terms of strengthening brands. I am among those who generally regard acquisitions with a great amount of skepticism. In my experience, most mergers lead to a bigger company and more market share, but seldom to the expected synergies, especially when they take place in mature markets where both companies in the merger have acquired a deep-rooted culture of their own.

Usually the companies you want to acquire are the evil competitors, the very people against which you have traditionally benchmarked and sought to differentiate yourself from, are suddenly on the same side. Foe turns into friend. This is not easy. In the case of Volvo and Scania, for example, the two fiercest competitors in the truck-building business were supposed overnight to become one company (with two brands). In the event, the European Union competition authorities stopped the merger on antitrust grounds.

Cultural problems are always difficult to handle, mostly because they are irrational and therefore hard to negotiate beforehand and then to handle in everyday situations after the deal is closed. Culture consists of values, and values are an important part of the Brand Code. The Code also includes other essential cultural components such as style, mission, and vision.

Sometimes acquisitions are necessary elements in building a good business; sometimes this is the only way to kill competition that threatens to make the business too small for everybody. When getting involved in acquisitions, it is very useful to have your own Brand Code documented. Then construct the Future Brand Code and the Brand Mind Space for the business you intend to acquire. And then compare them, piece by piece.

It is a very good 'investment' to sit down with your management team doing the same kind of exercise you did for your own company, trying to figure out the brand platform of the target company. I get many requests from companies to evaluate financially the brand they are about to buy. Naturally I do my best, but it is sometimes difficult since I very rarely if ever get all the information required to do a proper evaluation.

Instead of reaching a more or less fictional financial value, it is more important in my opinion to get a sense of how valuable the brand you are about to acquire could become for your future business situation, or not. Sometimes experienced businesspeople get carried away by the fact that they can get their hands on a very well-known brand name, without thinking what it really means to them in straight business terms. It might not be worth anything, because you actually have to kill it in order to promote your own, newer brand that stands for something different, and may be much more up to date.

While doing the brand platform of your acquisition target, you might not be able to get all the information you need to fill in the Brand Code or the Brand Mind Space exactly as you want it. Then, of course, you will have to guess a little. If you have a chance to sit down later with the people involved in the real one and check, you will be pretty close in any case.

How do you know from a branding (and maybe also from a cultural) point of view when it is right to make an acquisition?

The most important part is to check the sync between the brands on *style, mission, vision,* and *values.* Benefit and competence might be different, but maybe that is the whole point of the acquisition in the first place: to widen the product line and strengthen the position by competence and new product combinations. I would generally say that the vision and values are the most critical, as they are the most difficult to change. The style is easier to deal with; if you are clever you can take a little style from here and a little from there to combine in the new merged company. Style also changes with the times in any event. The mission of the acquired company should be at least in the neighborhood of your own mission. Once you have done this exercise you will be much better off in your negotiation.

Selecting partners with The Brand Code™

SOMETIMES PARTNERSHIPS ARE as important for your brand as acquiring another company and integrating it with your own. Strategic partnerships can be an important tool for shaping a brand.

Your partners say as much about your brand as your own products do. Associating yourself with the right kind of partner can lift the value of your brand significantly. When Siemens went into partnership with Porsche Design to produce prestige electrical appliances such as a toaster, a coffee maker, and a kettle, it lifted its brand value significantly in this market. Its products now enjoy the highest status.

Of course, Porsche would never have gone into partnership with a company that was unable to deliver the technical engineering necessary to make the product reliable and functional. In a partnership, the choice to enter is equally important to both parties. You could, for instance, think that to get into a partnership with a strong brand would always be good, but that's not necessarily the case.

If you are a weak brand yourself or stand for something that doesn't fit with the partner brand, then you are in trouble. The value of your brand will vanish and the strong brand will gain at your expense.

Even a strong brand is dependent on its partners. In fact, some brands have made partnerships a strategy, most typically the ingredient brands: Gore-Tex, Intel, Teflon, Nutrasweet, but also Virgin.

But for super-strong independent brands such as Disney, co-branding or brand partnership is also a strategy. Disney has successfully partnered with Kodak, Mattel, McDonald's, and Coca-Cola. The strategy seems to be to choose the leading brand in its field. Disney has a vice president of synergies reporting to the president, responsible for continually finding the best strategic partners to co-brand with.

Without a policy to find those partners, it can be extremely difficult to know which partner is the right one for you, and to know where to look for your partners. With your Brand Code it's much easier, in fact in your Brand Code you have your policy. And sometimes when you are approached by someone, it is much easier to say no if you can refer to such a policy. Usually a 'no' based on a Brand Code creates a great deal of respect for you as a company.

"Experience is not what
happens to you. It is what you do with
what happens to you."

Aldous Huxley

PERSONAL
BRANDING 4-D 4-U

4-D Leadership

BRANDING IS PERSONAL. Given the maelstrom of change and the profusion of demands, tomorrow's leaders are going to have to be special people. They are certainly going to be different to traditional leaders. I have identified four types of leadership for the future – the one that is most applicable to your company depends on the type of business you are in, and your company's position in the market.

The Leadership of Tomorrow

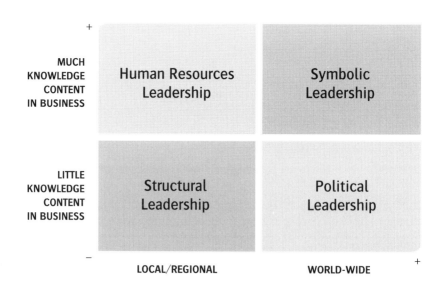

+

MUCH KNOWLEDGE CONTENT IN BUSINESS

Human Resources Leadership

Symbolic Leadership

LITTLE KNOWLEDGE CONTENT IN BUSINESS

Structural Leadership

Political Leadership

–

LOCAL/REGIONAL

WORLD-WIDE

+

The Structural Leader is a social architect whose leadership style is analysis and design – the focus is on structure, strategy, environment, implementation, experimentation, and adaptation. This leadership style is very important if you are in a product-based local or regional business.

The Human Resource Leader is a catalyst and servant whose leadership style is to support, advocate, and empower. Visible and accessible, these leaders increase participation, support, share information, and move decision making down into the organization. This is the leadership style successfully performed by managers in knowledge-based smaller businesses, such as regional consulting firms.

The Political Leader is an advocate, whose leadership style is coalition and consensus building. Able to clarify what they want and what they can get, they assess the distribution of power and interests; they build linkages to other stakeholders; they use persuasion first, then negotiation and coercion only if necessary. This style is important in manufacturing industries or commodity industries.

The Symbolic Leader is basically a prophet, whose leadership style is inspiration. Viewing organizations as a stage or theatre on which to play particular roles and present impressions, these leaders use symbols to capture attention; they try to frame experience by providing plausible interpretations of experiences; they discover and communicate a vision. This style is typically very important in industries with high knowledge content and worldwide distribution, for instance using the Internet.

In all these types of leadership the brand plays an important role:

For the Structural Leader, the brand signifies key values of product or service quality.

For the Human Resource Leader, the brand is a set of values and attitudes that are important to signify the relations inside the company and those between the company and its customers.

For the Political Leader, the brand is an important property and a tool for building alliances, merging businesses, and as an ingredient in marketing.

For the Symbolic Leader, the brand is everything; it contains the values and experiences that this type of leader needs to communicate the corporate mission efficiently and to build relevance in the market.

Intuition and knowledge about human behaviour will increasingly occupy the minds of tomorrow's managers. But at the same time, business managers will also continue to base their decisions on calculations, or mathematical relationships. In parallel with increasing acceptance of the importance of intuition and behaviour in management, there is an equally strong trend – or urge – for measuring quality parameters that were earlier perceived as impossible to quantify. That is why my methods emphasize new ways to quantify the subtleties of customers' perceptions of a brand.

The technology for quantifying quality parameters in all areas of business will boom in the new business culture. The moment that a new business idea based on intuition is valued or forecasted in dollars, it will become real. The new trend here forms a bridge between the old and the new paradigm, the new business culture realizing, accepting, and developing this need to quantify.

The individual above all

INDIVIDUALISM IS NOW the name of the game – in society as well as in the business. In 1989, the Berlin Wall – the emblem of collectivist shackles – crumbled and fell. Millions of people around the world watched on television as people power was unleashed on the symbol of authoritarian rule. In the eyes of many, it was a moment that defined a new world order – economic, political and social. Today, the Internet is undermining that other collectivist power base, the corporation. Today, every one of us has to be a brand in our own right.

The importance of this has to do with yourself, but also with the group or network of which you are a part. Paradoxically, the new economy is actually creating a new kind of collectivity, one based on individuality rather than conformity. That's the crucial difference. Uniqueness is king. Against this background, the need to brand yourself and to know what you stand for is quite obvious. It makes it easier for you to find out where you fit and how you will contribute to the group or network.

Who are you? Why are you different? What's your personality? How do you add value? These are the questions being asked by people who want to do business with you, employ you, or choose you as a member of a special project group. It is a question we all ask ourselves from time to time. It is in fact one of the most fundamental questions in human philosophy, the question of identity. In the Old Economy you could always lean on other identities. The school or university you went to, for example, was a form of identity, especially if it was a well-known brand like Oxford or Harvard. Or it could be the company you worked for – you could identify yourself by referring to a big corporation: 'I'm an IBMer,' or even 'I'm an ex-IBMer.'

But how helpful is that today? It might still be useful, but it is not decisive. We are less impressed by backgrounds than we used to be. What is really important in the New Economy is you, 'The Brand Yourself,' as Tom Peters put it in his 1997 book about the new rules of working life. In this new golden age of opportunity, what *you are* is the most important factor in professional life. It is a much more democratic society. People have more equal chances, and young people can *be somebody* without really growing up first. To do something on your own, to achieve something, to build something with the talent you've got, that's what counts now.

What is your mission in life? What is your style? How are you *different*? What is your talent? And what is your personal contribution, or benefit? What is your vision for yourself? Who are you going to be in 10–15 years from now? What are your values? What are your own rules of life? What is your motto, or your tag line, or your personal mantra? Or simply, what do you stand for? In the Old Economy you could borrow some ideas to stand for, political, educational, or social. Today it is more demanding. *You have to stand for something on your own*!

Like an actor, you have different roles, in different scenes. Work life used to be separate, but today your personal life is likely to be far more integrated with your professional life. In both areas people demand to know who you are. The relationship we all want to have with other people is built on knowing, liking, and accepting what they are in certain ways. It's when we don't know who we are dealing with that we get uncomfortable, we begin to make our own hypotheses of what that person might be. The uncertainty makes us unsure and suspicious. Just as we don't like corporations that we can't trust because we don't know exactly what they stand for, the same applies to individuals. There are equally good reasons for human beings and corporations to stand for something. And in the transparent, on-line world in which we now live, this is increasingly important.

Tom Peters has done much to establish the 'Brand You' concept. I'd like to go one step further by introducing you to an idea on how to create that 'Brand You' based on the principles of 4-D Branding. You can use the same approach to build a Brand Code for yourself and create your very own Brand Mind Space. It is an idea that returns the metaphor to its origins.

The 4-D Branding concept was built on the idea of creating an organic personality, a DNA, in an abstract organization for products or services. My approach is to recreate and simulate the mind work of a talented entrepreneur, but within management teams. The corporate branding metaphor can be used on ourselves, possibly to help create that very talented entrepreneur I was role-modelling in the first place. The purpose of this, of course, is to bring clarity and insight to the individual's mind, but there's another purpose as well. Through a clearer understanding of your personal brand, you can gauge your fit with the corporate brand.

How do you fit the company you work for?

IF THE COMPANY you work for doesn't fit you, you would probably like to know. It is in your own interest, as much as your employer's, to understand how well you match your company. In today's recruitment market these are very important issues. To get the *right* kind of talent, to attract people, to match people to your business, are top management issues. It is not so different to making an acquisition of another company. In both cases you have to know what everyone stands for.

There are several good reasons for wanting a good brand fit between employee and employer:

1. The brand is the core of the corporation, it is there for everybody to see.
2. The same questions that define the brand can easily be asked to define a person.
3. People are one of the greatest assets in a modern business, and also the single most important asset in building a brand, so to have one transparent value system for both the company as a whole and the individuals working for that company is as close to the entrepreneurial idea of a brand as possible.
4. The brand is the differentiation code of the company as well as for the individual. This means that the individual should not be exactly the same as the company (that is, if you don't want an army of soldiers in uniform). The talents of individuals should complement the company, within the framework of the Brand Code. This is a common problem when hiring talent; if they are outside of your framework, it doesn't matter how talented they are!

Creating your personal brand

THE PROCESS OF PERSONAL branding basically follows the same path as the process described in this book to build a platform for the corporate brand. I will go through it again briefly to comment on the differences.

The 4-D Branding Process for individuals consist of these three parts:

Brand Future Scenario
Brand Mind Space
Brand Code

The *Brand Future Scenario* will help you to sort out what scenarios you hold as a background to your own brand, what you want to stand for. This is fundamentally what many people do when they choose a career path, trying to figure out where the best possibilities on the job market will arise. The problem is that you don't usually do this in a structured and profound way.

The model of cross-impact analysis, which is a part of the Brand Future Scenario method, is valuable if you want a more detailed and refined picture of your own future. In the new worlds of opportunity at the crossroads of two trends, a totally new profession can arise, such as when the health food trend and the ecological trend combine, creating businesses and opportunities. You could do this particular workshop together with somebody else. The task is to collect impulses and ideas from your own mind as well as possibly being stimulated by articles in trend magazines. Sort the trends out and discuss their probability, trying to the most probable crossing points and create new worlds. This is a fun and social thing to do together.

The *Brand Mind Space* describes the perception of *you* in the minds of other people. As with the Brand Mind Space for a company or a product brand, there are in reality as many Brand Mind Spaces as there are people trying to figure out who you are and what you stand for. When you do it for yourself, though, you work with the desired perception of You, or how you'd *like* to be perceived in the minds of other people. That's why it's such a good idea to do that before you do the Brand Code, which is what you finally *want* to stand for.

Personal Brand Mind

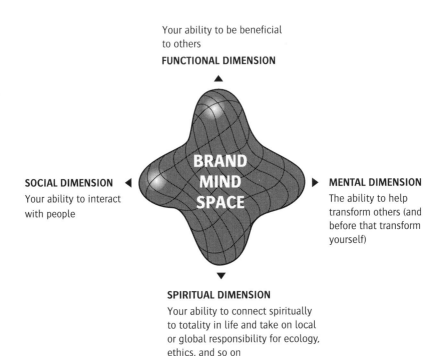

Your ability to be beneficial to others
FUNCTIONAL DIMENSION

SOCIAL DIMENSION
Your ability to interact with people

BRAND MIND SPACE

MENTAL DIMENSION
The ability to help transform others (and before that transform yourself)

SPIRITUAL DIMENSION
Your ability to connect spiritually to totality in life and take on local or global responsibility for ecology, ethics, and so on

FUNCTIONAL U

This might be the part of your personal Brand Mind Space that is the most traditional part of your personal brand. The Functional Dimension answers the question, how can you be beneficial to others? And of course, this means how you can be perceived to be beneficial, not necessarily what good you actually do. We are talking about you as a brand here, the perceived reality, not necessarily the real reality of what you actually are. You might feel that you have many hidden strengths in your personality, but if you are not able to communicate that picture of you, from a personal branding point, those strengths are non-existent.

The functional side of your perceived personality has to do with your professional and formal abilities or skills. These can, of course, be based on your education and formal training. But they can also be the subject of your talent.

A favourite word for the functional dimension of a person is competence, a blend of knowledge and experience. The functional dimension is also about productivity in economic terms. What is your product; how can you be beneficial to a company (or partner); what is your output in a more traditional sense? The functional dimensions are about your deliverables as a person, mainly in your work life but just as easily be in other areas of activity, such as you as a Brand in your golf club, or in your family, or in any other organization.

The whole point of thinking about what functional dimension you want to hold in other people's perception is that this will make you focus on how to be *different*, and then how to *dramatize* that difference when you communicate yourself to others. A typical functional dimension could be 'I like Thomas because he is such a good analytical thinker, and such a good presenter of very complex issues.'

People with very clear and strong functional dimensions include professionals such as lawyers, doctors, and specialists in IT – clearly valuable for everybody on a personal or corporate level.

SOCIAL U

In personal branding the social dimension is about your social skills, your ability to organize and lead people, but maybe even more importantly the role model you are in other people's minds. The clearest indicator that you have a strong social dimension is if you are someone whose name other people might drop.

The extremely successful person with charisma is, like a good corporate brand, able to create a cult. A popular word for the social dimension is leadership. To have a strong social dimension is to be a naturally sociable person; a person who is invited to make other people feel good, a funny, or amiable, interesting character; someone admired by others.

The typical profession for a person with dominant social dimensions in personal branding is the team leader in any organization or a salesperson; many people in sales have the talent of being the one others wait for before they start a meeting ... or a party.

MENTAL U

The extreme on this dimension is the guru. The mental dimension is all about the ability to *transform* other people, to have them develop personally as a result of your contact. The basis for this is that you have been able to transform yourself (maybe as a result of a contact with someone else with a strong mental dimension). You will probably have some kind of inner stability, conviction – even enlightenment.

To have a strong mental dimension in other people's perception means that you have a talent for creating rapport with others, and you most probably show empathy, the ability to put yourself easily in other people's shoes. You are a philosopher of a kind. 'I like Sandy because she really listens to me and gives me new insights about myself' could be a typical expression of the mental dimension.

Typical professions for a full mental dimensional personal brand include corporate seniors, and all kinds of therapists, consultants, and mental trainers, but they could include people generally regarded as 'wise,' such as some very talented management advisers.

SPIRITUAL U

The spiritual dimension is about being connected with totality in life. This might sound weird, and this is probably the most difficult of the four dimensions to grasp. Almost all of us are searching for a mission, a role in society. So the fact that some of us instinctively take on a responsibility for something larger than ourselves, or even the company or organization we work for, is completely natural, and important for our own self-respect and identity. The spiritual dimension is about serving higher purposes than the traditional professional. It involves the capacity to contribute to everybody's welfare and to public development.

Some people have a talent and a motivation for this. Of course, you can have a profession connected with it, such as social workers, priests, or environmentalists. But many people have the capacity to do this within their existing work or as a part of their private time. Every community, as well as every company, needs these idealists, who form a very important part of success, mostly because they have a larger view on things, they are visionaries and future drivers.

To figure out your potential on the spiritual dimension you have to ask yourself what is it in life that makes you the most satisfied. If the answer is something tied to local or social responsibility, then you have a good spiritual dimension to exploit.

A typical perception of the spiritual dimension could be: 'I like Steven because of his passion to develop a better and simplified IT infrastructure.'

Matching your brand

THE PERFECT TOOL to match your own brand with the brand company you work for, or are about to work for, is *the Brand Code*. To use the Brand Code from a personal branding perspective, you start with the Brand Code of your company.

If your company doesn't have one, you will have to construct one. To do that you need to read websites, annual reports, corporate presentations, and recruitment ads, but you can also ask specific questions of responsible people in the company in order to be able to fill in the six inputs: benefit, competence, style, mission, vision, and values. You might have to guess or estimate. You might also find an expression that could serve as the Brand Code Core Message (the one in the middle of the Brand Code).

Once you have the company Brand Code, it's time to do your own Brand Code. You do it in the same way, using your Brand Mind Space as a framework.

PRODUCT/BENEFIT

Looking at yourself as a product or service, you have to ask yourself what is the greatest benefit you bring to your organization? (Use the functional u in the Brand Mind Space for guidance.) If your product, your competence and professionalism, are totally different from the company's product, then you seriously have to ask yourself what this means. Does it mean that you will be employed to complement the company, doing something that the company badly needs? If you are a true professional in your area, you will probably create respect and be beneficial. But it can also be a true mismatch. Ask yourself whether your ambitions in life are totally different, or not, from what seems to be this company's business. If you find that you are too far apart, and that they would not respect you for your specialty, then seek a job elsewhere.

POSITIONING

What is it that you do best? Why are you better than, or different from, others? And how does that fit with the positioning of the company in its market? Let's say that the company's positioning is to be different in the way it distributes and services its customers, and your difference is in being a very good researcher. Again, here a mismatch isn't necessarily negative, as long as the company appreciates the need for your expertise. But if it needs only people who do what they are best at, and you don't like to position yourself like that, then you are in trouble here from day one. On the other hand, if the company really needs your brand to deliver its difference, and you feel you will be valued for it, then it may be the right place for you.

To find out, you might have to check what your colleagues do, how they are positioned. This is usually easy to discover. Find out exactly what you are expected to do and in what context. Are there other people with similar sorts of positioning to yours that you will have to compete with? How do you rate your positioning in relation to them? Will you be valuable at all? How would your differentiation help the company to differentiate? That is the key question. If you are a very specialized and a very good sales-person, your differentiation might do wonders for the company. If you feel you can do it, go for it. If you are doubtful, then look for a company in which your specialization might be a better fit.

STYLE

When I talk about style, I mean the perception that you create – or want to create. It is more about the direct impression you make, your attitude and the feelings you create among others, whereas the 'values' are your deeper personality.

Of course, it's good when your personal style fits well with the company culture. Check with yourself how much pain it would take for you to ad-just. If you feel that merely minor adjustments are needed, than go for it.

MISSION

The mission is about purpose and your role in society, or your benefit to the community. The company's mission may be one of your most important criteria for choosing an employer. If your own mission demands meaning and importance to humanity, then of course the company you work for should have the same leverage. This may come in stages, and finally pro-duce the meaning you expect for yourself in life.

But be critical when you make such a judgment; do the managers really share a commitment to do what they say they will do? If they seem to stand behind their mission with commitment, and you yourself have a larger expectation, a more demanding and generous mission in your own Brand Code, it could still be OK. If the company has a broader mission than your own, it may challenge your mission, which is great. Obviously the nature of the mission is important and should be in sync with you.

If the company's mission totally fails to excite you, then your decision is easy, at least from a mission standpoint; you should not get involved.

VISION

See yourself 10–15 years from now. What picture comes to mind? Now do the same for your company. How well do the visions work together? A company with an exciting and large vision, larger than your own but able to accommodate it, will present you with a good challenge. Try to find out if this big vision amounts to more than just words, if it has commitment and realism behind it.

If the company's vision is weak and your own vision stronger and larger, then beware. A potential conflict awaits you down the line, but you might still consciously want to use this company as a stepping-stone in your career.

VALUES

This is usually the most important factor when matching your own brand with the brand of the company. The values are the rules of life, the deeper personality, the elements that will make the brand as trustworthy as a friend, and you as trustworthy as a good brand. You need to be careful here. Try to find out what the real values are; check and double check. If your own values clash with the values of the company, that should act as a warning.

The wording might be different, but the meaning is what counts. Some of your values might be missing and you may be able to live with that. But if some of the company's values are questionable, then you should definitely back out.

When you are matching your own Brand Code with the Brand Code of the company, you should pay particular attention to the items on the right-hand side: mission, vision, and values. Benefit, competence and style – a mismatch here can be fruitful and even necessary. If you are able to offer a different product to the company you work for, and have a different competence, this might be exactly what is needed. A different style might be refreshing. But if your own mission, vision and values and those of the company are miles apart, then you will probably have trouble ahead.

Are you ready for personal branding?

PERSONAL BRANDING LIKE THIS involves defining who you really are, clarifying yourself. Many people don't like this, they prefer to hide. Some also have a natural talent for defining and communicating what they stand for. They are like talented musicians, playing the music by ear. Some find it more difficult; they need the music written down, they need a process of self-reflection, which for most people will be the introduction to inner self-development.

The benefit of this process is that you have to explore and express your own view of yourself and how you actually want to be perceived. This is something we seldom do for ourselves, instead letting others describe us.

We almost never think of ourselves in a structured way, and very few of us deliberately try to manage and implement our own desired personality in a systematic way. Are you really ready for personal branding?

8

TEN COMMANDMENTS FOR A BRAND WITH A FUTURE

As a summary, I would like to outline the 10 most important rules for creating brands that will be successful and profitable, as well as building value for the long-term. It is of course always difficult to choose exactly 10; maybe it should be 15 or just 5. These 10 represent my basic views on how branding will evolve in the next 10 years or so.

1 A brand with a future is created in a person's mind (not by the product or service itself).

The traditional view of branding is product and service oriented. It is very much focused on the unique benefit of the product. But the world is changing and is full of examples of extremely virtual phenomena, which do not meet the criteria of the classical product or service. The emergent brands do not have the substance that we are used to attaching to a classic brand. A product or service without a recognized brand is pure utility and availability for the buyer, and can as such be replaced. A brand set in someone's mind is much more unique and, most importantly, individual.

2 A brand with a future must stand for something, be different (not necessarily pleasing to everybody).

'It is better to be something to someone, than nothing to everyone' the saying goes, and that is very much a truth in branding. The traditional brand does not want to turn anybody down; usually it is a brand for a mass-market product defined to attract a mass audience. The problem with that is, of course, that the brand becomes emotionally very shallow. Meeting the new individual audience, the recipe for success is to stand for something special, to have a philosophy and to be different not only in features but in attitude. Such a brand will create brand fans, or even brand groupies, that by sheer loyalty will not only stand by your brand for themselves, they will also enthusiastically introduce it to others. Also, standing for something different in attitudes and values is often easier than maintaining staying power in product or service differences.

3 A brand with a future is involving like a dear friend.

Friendship is one of the easiest ways to understand the subtleties of a brand. If you close your eyes and think about a friend and then try to describe what that friendship is all about, you are very much in the same situation as describing what a very good brand is for you. The words will fail, because the experience is beyond words. To create a brand like that you not only have to stand for something special, you also have to be involving. And to be involving as a brand, you can copy how you would be involving as a friend. Personal attention, recognition, giving nice little surprises, and doing exciting things with your friend would most probably improve your friendship, and the same goes for branding. You might additionally find a common cause in which to engage passionately, and you will then have the most perfect recipe for success as a brand builder.

4 A brand with a future is always regarded as the company's most valuable asset.

The brand is not just a marketing tool, it is quite often the critical 'substance' of your company, yet it is not formally seen as such. Most of us recognize this, but we seem to ignore it. The reason is that the official system we live in has not been able to adjust to the change. Other, much less important assets have historically received much greater attention, things like property, machinery, and technology, assets that are annually audited. So-called human capital is an asset not yet officially valued, but much discussed, and still the value of all these assets usually depends more on the strength of the brand as an asset than on anything else. We have all witnessed how a weak brand, losing trust in its markets, makes the rest of a 'solid' company worth very little.

Of course, this will change over time. Auditors will not forever accept auditing just a small and less important part of a company, and the legal system will not accept having the dominant part of a company value outside of the system, so to speak. The new generation of managers already acknowledge the change, and their focus on their company's brand, or brands, is totally different from that held by the old generation of managers.

5 A brand with a future is used by management to drive the company.

There is no tool better than the brand for uniting the forces and the stakeholders inside and around your company. Leading a company today seems like a mission impossible; so many conflicting interests, so much ambition, in so many different directions. Managing is all about focusing mental energies. Any leakage of energy, any unproductive connections, will cause a loss of voltage, affecting the power of the brand on the market. And conversely, a powerful brand in the marketplace will charge up not only the people working inside the company but also the owners and public opinion.

This is a true chicken-and-egg situation, but what is good is that it is very much within your control as a manager. You can start the process from the inside, you don't have to wait for something else to happen first. Start with setting up a Brand Code and use it as a universal instrument of change!

6 A brand with a future is crystal clear about its role in the marketplace.

There was a time when you could be a little bit of everything. It was a nice time, because you didn't have to say no to anything; if you weren't sure what to do, or decide, you just said 'yes' or 'maybe'! If you look at the structure of the traditional enterprise you still see the remains of that. But most of the world's leading companies have focused their businesses, driven by internationalization and tougher competition.

You now have to do very much the same thing with your brand. You not only have to focus on which business you are in, but also what role in that business you want to play. Are you a *production brand*, with unique know-how in methods or technology? Then you might take the consequences of that and build an ingredient brand, not locking yourself into distributing to one customer or channel only, but co-branding with everybody filling the criteria of your Brand Code. Or maybe you are *relation brand* that has a very special knowledge of your customers and a unique distribution platform. Then you might take the consequences of this and build your brand into a meeting place, a portal, in which you should have the freedom to choose any production brand, or any source of production. This new focus on the role of your brand in your business is driven by the transparency of the market, which in turn is induced by the Internet.

7 A brand with a future encourages creativity, not least among its customers.

Interactivity and creativity form the name of the new game. A future brand has to be experienced as interactive and 'owned' and somehow created by its customers and company employees. Its products and services can always be improved, and continual improvement is the cornerstone of quality, but what is new is really putting the customer to work on this.

The forerunners in this are include the software industry, which invented the most ingenious creativity and customer activity instrument of them all – the 'beta test.' Having beta testers not only helps the software producer to make a better, bug-free product, it produces prestige, ambassadors, and 'insiders,' and above all it turns critics into supporters, all by using the tool of creativity. Human beings can't resist a creative challenge – if you ask someone to solve a problem that you have, you have the start of a possible friendship. Another software example is Linus Torvalds and Linux, a gigantic creative joint venture in which all participators feel like owners, which they are in a way because no one really owns this software – it is freeware.

Inspire yourself by these examples, and turn your brand into a real concern for a lot of people.

8 A brand with a future enjoys alliances with other brands (rather than maintaining exclusivity at all costs).

The traditional brands were very anxious not to involve themselves with other brands. And possibly rightly so, if you consider that few of them were really brands in the way we now view the term. They were more or less just trademarks or very shallow brands. But strong brands, standing for something special, distinctive, based on deeper values, brands like that have nothing to fear from connecting themselves to other brands, if there is a match in Brand Codes. Ingredient branding, co-branding, and co-branding activities are the latest way to explore the mindspace landscape of values that might be held in common for many brands. Sharing this common ground can make everybody a winner.

It doesn't really matter which is the strongest of the brands involved to begin with. A strong brand might strengthen its brand by co-branding with a less strong one that stands for interesting or refreshing values. And a small brand with a distinctive and exciting brand code can definitely be a winner if it joins a big and well-known one, again provided that the Brand Codes are not critically conflicting.

Every brand has everything to gain by exposing itself and connecting with the right things, in the right environment and the right kind of people. Your Brand Code will be able to help you check out what's right for your brand.

9 A brand with a future is best protected by itself (rather than by trademark laws).

Traditionally, trademark legal protection has been very important for protecting the brand. But in recent years, with internationalization and the transparency of the Web, it has become very difficult to control all the legal aspects of a brand. Many established brand owners have had many problems with websites taken in their name and so on.

That legal trademark protection may become less important in the future. In a transparent Web-driven culture, consumers will look more for inner values in the brand. The new consumer will know who is behind a certain brand, where something is manufactured, how responsible the company is, and so on. Any fraud or deviation will be more easily discovered, but also reported to other consumers on the Web. The deeper relationship with the customer, the total information that the customer will have, makes it meaningless to create bad copies or imitations. A copy or imitation always builds on the lack of knowledge that it is fraud. Of course, a perfect fraud will still be confusing until it is discovered and reported on the Web. A fraud against a brand that maintains a base of loyal customers may indeed further strengthen the bond between the customers and the brand under attack.

A distinct philosophy brand with a good Brand Code and a community of brand friends will be more important for protecting the brand than any legal protection of the trademark.

10 A brand with a future is a vehicle for the transfer of both value and values.

The tenth and last of the commandments wraps up the nine before – and the book as a whole for that matter – and it connects with the first commandment, giving branding a more general, economic, and philosophical base to stand on.

The purpose of the brand is to be a vehicle for transferring both value and values. From one product generation to the next. From one product to its derivatives, also called line extension. From one kind of a product to another kind, also called brand extension. Between company and product, and vice versa. Between the company, product, and its customers, and between buying occasions. And between the company and staff, owners and public opinion.

Why is this so important? First, the brand is not only an economic but also a philosophical mechanism. It is not just about money, it is about culture and humanity as well. And in the future development of the brand, the philosophical aspect will be essential to produce economic results. In the years to come we may well see a change in business attitude and thinking, from the value chain to a chain of values.

Notes

1 S I Hill, J McGrath and S Dayal, 'How to brand sand', *Strategy & Business*, Second Quarter 1998
2 K Keller, 'The Brand Report Card', *Harvard Business Review*, Jan – Feb 2000
3 Interbrand, based on *Financial Times* index over the 350 largest corporations in UK
4 Virgin Group literature
5 E Schonfeld, 'Betting on the Boomers', *Fortune*, 1995